BUNKIE EMERITUS

Climbing Up the Downside of Dementia with My Mom

A Commentary on the Effects of Alzheimer's

Carole Cash Stemley

VANTAGE PRESS
New York

Excerpts from "God Happens!" previously published in *The Christian Index* © March 2003 by the CME Publishing House, Memphis, TN, reprinted with permission.

Cover design by Elaine F. Adger

FIRST EDITION

Published by Vantage Press, Inc.
419 Park Ave. South, New York, NY 10016

Manufactured in the United States of America
ISBN: 0-533-14796-4

Library of Congress Catalog Card No.: 2003098264

0 9 8 7 6 5 4 3 2 1

This entire effort is dedicated
to the spiritual personae
of the two people
I love most
and
whose lives I cherish
with unlimited gratitude:

My Mother
Carrie Mae Bryant Grove
(1913–2000)

And Grandmother
Lola Mae Starks Grove
(1897–1984)

Contents

Acknowledgments

The emotional journey from the first word through the final page of this book was supported by a number of good friends and well-wishers to whom I am grateful. I am also especially indebted to the following persons for their assistance, confidence, encouragement, and tolerance; Mrs. Elaine Adger, Dr. Thomas E. Adger, Mrs. Thelma Favors, Mrs. Louise Gaddy, Mr. Major Gaddy, Mr. Raymond Gambrell, Mrs. Clara Hayley, Mrs. Fredericka Hurley, Mrs. Lillian Johnson, Miss Monica Lewis, Mrs. Edith Linsey, Mrs. Mae Linsey, Bishop Nathaniel Linsey, Miss Ruth Pruitt, Mrs. Ruth Reed, Mrs. Earline (Poppye) Wood, and Mr. Thomas E. Wood, Jr.

Introduction

Children are notorious for not cleaning up their rooms and not doing their homework for the next school day. They conveniently use "I forgot" as an excuse because that reason is forgiven as easily as it is given. Adults are more sophisticated. They forget where they place their car keys or eyeglasses and declare them lost, only to find them within minutes. These situations involve incidental circumstances under which things can afford to be forgotten.

Forgetfulness, as "to err," is also human. However, some things in life are not expected to be forgotten. For instance, we are expected to remember our names and where we live. That expectation is one of the many rules or standards that separates normal mentality from abnormal mentality.

Social expectations also apply to our expressed behavior; people are expected to act and react in a certain way. Who among us with a grain of sanity would suddenly stand alone during a regular church service and loudly sing, "Mary Had a Little Lamb," or perceive such behavior as being normal?

Habitual forgetfulness and unexpected displays of senseless behavior sometimes indicate a possibility of dementia, a relentless psychological mishap that covers several mental disorders. A common type of dementia, especially among the elderly, is Alzheimer's disease. From the time a person's mind is changed by effects of Alzheimer's, there is no known cure for mental recovery.

One of my earliest and most remembered real-life experiences of seeing someone showing symptoms of dementia involved a woman known on the streets as "Big Bertha." During the late 1950s, Big Bertha was often noticed on weekends as she aimlessly walked around the same area on the Atlanta University (AU) campus in Atlanta, Georgia. Supposedly, Big Bertha was a former AU student who failed to receive a master's degree because she missed the deadline for submitting her thesis by a few minutes. Spectators routinely ignored or dismissed Big Bertha's presence as the lady who had "lost her mind."

Almost forty years after I first saw Big Bertha, dementia became a much more serious and personal encounter for me. A small number of our family friends and my former coworkers were stricken with Alzheimer's. My mom's stepsister showed signs of dementia in the form of Sundowner's syndrome. Dementia, with complications from Alzheimer's disease, was officially documented as the secondary cause of my mother's death.

The experience of being my mom's only caregiver in our home made me realize dementia was much more complicated than I thought. I determined soon that dementia, especially Alzheimer's, is a drastic debilitating and dehumanizing mental disorder. Over a period of weeks, months, and even years, the mind undergoes a weakening process until completely retiring from the social, personal, and emotional realities of life. Yet, throughout this weakening process, the mind seems to struggle against the doom of becoming a permanent dysfunction.

Alzheimer's is a come-and-go disorder of the mind. There is no consistent schedule for episodes of this demented behavior. Though I became accustomed to specific episodes, my eventual relief was the surprise of "episodic freedom" for a brief span of consecutive days, and then, just hours.

As my mom's bout with dementia became more critical, I also realized that my emotional survival was not an option. It was a **must** that became easier with faith and humor. "Bunkie Emeritus" shares the significance of those two factors in related segments about our lives and is intended to increase public awareness about the onset and impact of dementia.

Erosion of the human mind has to be the greatest theft of human dignity. Out of respect for their previous ability to function with mental normality, my sentiment is that all victims of dementia should be granted "emeritus" status. The entire presentation of *Bunkie Emeritus* is based on that opinion and written from a personal and nonclinical perspective.

May the climb for all caregivers become easier . . .
Bunkie is my mother!

Part One

Once upon Our Mountain

Bunkie, Mama, and Me

Bunkie is my mother because she told me so. We met the first day of my prenatal existence, and she was the only one of my two biological parents that I ever knew. From the time my baby instincts kicked in and my infantile mind developed instant recall ability, I never doubted or forgot who my mother was. I am sure of that because the mother is the female parent who feeds the baby and smiles face to face with the baby until the baby finally says "mama" in some unknown language. Nevertheless, Bunkie continued to introduce herself to me as my mother a lot of times during my growing up years. She did it privately and publicly.

The more I think about it, all mothers in the neighborhood did the same thing to their children. They also banded together as wardens. If one mother was away from her duty post, all the other mothers remained more organized than the guards at Buckingham Palace. They always assumed their positions as tribal leaders and flaunted the parental fad of their generation.

Sometimes, as a precaution to what she might do, Bunkie also urged me to never forget that she was my mother. She usually issued that warning as the condition by which I would stay alive. So much passion was in her voice on those occasions that neither of us took time to think about my life ending any other way than by her hands. I last challenged her parental role in my life when

I was a sophomore in college. Again, she spared my life with that same warning while making me a true believer. Once my teenage years were out of the way, we bonded more and more and shared the typical ups and downs of a positive mother-daughter relationship for almost half a century.

For as long as I live, I am Bunkie's direct link to human life. Her title role in my life remains unchanged because, from the days of my youth, she constantly declared that she would be my mother for as long as she lived. As the extension of her life form, I find delight in honoring her declaration. Just as "a rose by any other name is a rose," Bunkie's present tense as my mother by any other time is her present tense. Therefore, Bunkie *is* my mother because she lives in my heart.

Bunkie was a native of Hart County, Georgia, and reared by her mother and stepfather. Her father was drowned accidentally when she was a "babe in arms." Born a Bryant, she grew up with her stepfather's last name as Carrie Mae Grove. Our attraction to a TV commercial in the early 1970s led to the two of us calling each other "Bunkie." Sometimes we pulled rank; she was Bunkie, Sr., and I was Bunkie, Jr. Until sharing Bunkie as a nickname, I always addressed my mom by her first name. Her mother was "Mama" in our household of three. Bunkie was an only child and a parent of one child; I had none.

Mama never joined in the trivia of calling either of us Bunkie, not that she was against using nicknames. Along with more than half her brothers and sisters, Mama grew up being called by her nickname. Though most of her ten siblings died before I was born, their nicknames were used frequently in family conversations. I was often confused when their real names and nicknames were used in the same conversation.

Mama was affectionately called "Moddie," with a short "O" sound, by older family members and friends. That spelling is probably incorrect, and I cannot begin to come close to spelling other family nicknames. But "Bunkie," I can do. That nickname is the only one that my mom and I ever had.

Between Bunkie and Mama, I enjoyed the best of two worlds. It was the same as one world with a twin. Mama and Bunkie were my immediate worlds. They provided me with a loving, clean, and safe home environment. Biological ownership and making final decisions about my life were the only rights that only one of them had in their reign over me. For the most part, however, those rights never made any difference to or for me. But for the sake of maternal reality, Bunkie—again—is my mother.

Bunkie and Mama often expressed opposing views, with my mom being more analytical, cautious, and traditional. I grew up as a mixture of their personalities. My grandmother and mother had different preferences in several areas. I rather enjoyed the task of choosing between them, especially when it came to food. Both of them were excellent cooks with different food preferences. I leaned more toward my grandmother's cooking style, down to the fried chicken and blackberry cobblers. Since Mama was more fashionable, I preferred that she buy my clothes.

The two of them were quite actively involved as church members and quick to disagree on church issues. Occasionally, I was drawn into those disagreements as their source of support or proof. However, if I feared for my life in choosing sides, I would have a sudden and severe case of amnesia.

5

My grandmother was my primary parent for almost ten years because my mom was working out of town. During those years, I was a major cause for some of their "entertaining" feuds. Once they started, regardless of the cause, I made myself as scarce as possible. I only hung around to eavesdrop when my personal desires or freedoms were at risk. Mama was more liberal with my social life. When they reached a settlement that I could accept, I would return on the scene to reap whatever benefits I could salvage.

One time, their compromise was the beginning of a tradition that lasted more than twenty years. Bunkie always baked a chocolate cake for my birthday. My grandmother, knowing that I also loved German chocolate cake, began baking a German chocolate cake for me to have on my birthday as well. The few times when I was living out of town, both birthday cakes came in the mail. As previously implied, Bunkie and Mama were the best of two worlds, and both worlds were mine—all mine!

Unfortunately, there were a few times when reaching a decision between them about my welfare was not an easy job to do. In those instances, I took advantage of both sides with a routine maneuver. I would simply change my request for whatever or withdraw it altogether. But their conversation would never end with my decision. Most times, they would continue for an hour or longer, debating or just wondering why I changed my mind. Those situations usually had a two-against-one ending, with my grandmother and me being in the two-spot.

Bunkie, Mama, and I belonged to each other and always supported one another in times of our joy and pain. We were "the three generations" who traveled together a lot, liked the same television programs, joked around with each other, and had one surgery apiece.

Bunkie and I shared the experience of having a thyroidectomy a year apart. Though my swollen thyroid gland was discovered a few months before Bunkie's, she had surgery first. My surgery had been delayed because the nature of my thyroid condition required a substantial period of preliminary treatment, but Bunkie's thyroid problem was more severe. Our surgeon jokingly reminded us that I had wanted Bunkie to be operated on first to test his surgical skills and my chance of survival. His full implication was that I had sacrificed my mother's life to him as a guinea pig.

Mama's surgery, which involved removal of a hernia, was at least twenty years before ours. In each case, neither of us felt physically or emotionally threatened by the idea of undergoing surgery. As fast healers, we could have been back in our daily swing of things within a week because our recoveries were so brief. But each of us took a little bit longer, just to be on the safe side. In my case, it was a matter of enjoying all the doting attention Bunkie and Mama showered on me.

From an individual perspective, Mama was the neatest and most energetic among us three. She kept our home spotless. Hopefully, she is too busy in heaven to look down and see it any time soon. Bunkie was a procrastinator and the most nonassuming. The *earliest* she ever filed her income taxes, with the exception of two times, was April 15th and, most times, far into the P.M. hours. I was the most organized and time-conscious.

Mama was the dwarf at barely five feet. Bunkie was tall, but I was the beanstalk, standing at 5 feet 10 inches. Each of us had proportionate weight, with Mama and Bunkie outweighing me by fifty pounds or more in our adult lives, but the weight looked good. Mama loved flowers and used her green thumb to maintain our back and front lawns as a picture of beauty. I truly hope God has her real busy in heaven. There's a lot of earthly disorder that she just does not need to see. At least, the plot she maintained as her vegetable garden is neatly mowed with the remainder of the back lawn.

We were quite a skilled threesome. Mama and Bunkie were non-certified paramedics who had a remedy for any ailment. Time and time again, they would override prescriptions of professionally trained doctors. Early one morning, I returned home from the hospital with my sprained ankle and brand new wooden crutches. Later in the day, Mama noticed that I continued to show the same pain as I did before going to the emergency room. So she made a red dirt pack, which may have been mixed with vinegar, and applied it to my ankle. The pack brought relief within minutes. A couple of hours is more truthful.

Bunkie was a make-it-yourself type. She reconstructed all kinds of stuff with glue and tape. I was the electrician and plumber.

Their personal leisure activities had nothing in common with mine. Bunkie enjoyed sewing and, for years, made her own outfits. She also made my high school graduation dress. All the girls in my graduation class, as was the custom, had to have their dresses made by the same pattern. I was so lucky to have a mother who was a home economics major in college.

Mama could sew well also. She made a lot of patchwork quilts. I, on the other hand, almost flunked sewing in high school after all the needle-threading I did for my mom and grandmother. I mean I had no sewing skill at all. There was no interest on my part either, but I tried. My classmates had moved on to making skirts, pants, and blouses while I was still working on the pot holder. The semester ended before I got to the second of our required class projects. We had a total of four. My interests were in piano, but I was far more skilled, trained, and interested in swimming, tennis, and, much later in life, bowling. I was the most "street involved" of the family. That's where I stayed, in the streets, even when I came home for holiday breaks. One time, because my presence was hardly seen at home, Mama called me her house guest.

On a more personal note, Mama married three times. The first two marriages were very brief. Her marriage of thirty years to my mom's stepfather held the longest record among us. Each of her marriages ended with the death of her spouse. When Bunkie and my dad did their quick split, Bunkie resumed her maiden name and never thought about courting or marriage again. After a great twenty-year on-and-off again love affair with a former professor of mine, we married in 1984. Our marriage was strained from the beginning because of the commuting distance between Atlanta and my husband's home in Oakland, California. We obtained a dissolution sixteen months later. Before our marriage, we broke up when he left Georgia to work at Grambling State University in Louisiana; almost one thousand miles closer than Oakland. It's evident that we didn't "go figure."

"The three generations," as we were often called because we were together so much, was our image for a long time. We were a moderately attractive and intelligent trio. The timing of our retirements provided us more quality time with each other. Before locating in Atlanta in 1947, Mama lived on her farm as a homemaker. In 1955, she retired from one of the Atlanta downtown clothing stores. She worked there as a maid on the office floor. Bunkie ended her thirty-nine years of teaching in Georgia with her retirement in 1977 from the Atlanta public school system. I retired from the same system in 1992.

Bunkie and I had graduate degrees, but Mama read with much better understanding and greater retention. She had a sixth grade education and used it the same way she did a one-dollar bill; she stretched it to the max! Bunkie taught me the value of establishing and maintaining good credit, and Mama showed me how to manage money.

We led simple lives on modest incomes. But our bonds of determination, love, strength, support, and trust made us quite wealthy and content with life. We were a family sustained by our Christian values and faith in God. We always had everything we needed and accumulated a family of genuine friends over the years. Our personality differences only added spice to our lives. In 1984, Bunkie and I were reduced to "two generations." Mama died that year on August 28th.

Between the best of my two worlds with Bunkie and Mama, I learned to navigate life with God. The transmission of that knowledge was my greatest inheritance. Good health was also a part of my natural inheritance; I am as healthy as they were at my age. Maybe, by divine intervention, I can further the image of our trio as an heir of their life span. Both of them died at the age of eighty-seven. My greatest joy as their survivor is being sustained by the memories we created during our lifetime together.

By Word, Deed, and Faith

A few days after the terrorist attack on America, September 11, 2001, I joined four friends for lunch. All of us were former high school classmates who would celebrate our forty-fifth class reunion the next year. In the course of our "professional" analysis of September 11, we suddenly changed our mood of seriousness to one of profound silliness. Silliness, for us, had been our main claim to fame for years and a binding tie of our friendship. We focused on a classroom prank that had been played on another classmate during our civics class when we were eighth graders. This incident had been recalled and laughed about many times over the years.

On the day of this particular incident, our civics teacher had lectured on the three historic battles of Atlanta and compared them to other major events of warfare. Following his brilliant lecture, our teacher asked this classmate, a male student, to summarize a main detail of World War I. Knowing all the while that the student had not been paying attention, the teacher allowed him to ask us, his compassionate classmates (not!), for help. Finally, while being coaxed, our classmate managed with several pauses and a bit of uncertainty to repeat the information being fed to him as the answer: "France got mad because Germany tried to fry Turkey in Greece with Chile." The class erupted in chaotic laughter. Our teacher left the room to laugh in solitude. The poor boy never had a clue.

My memory of that prank also includes my mom's reaction when I first told her about the incident. She laughed a bit and began what was probably her two-millionth lecture to me on character. The moral (as she always made well known) of that particular lecture was, "If you don't know something and know you don't know, don't *ever ever* let anybody else cause you to know less than what you already don't know." My mom and I continued to talk and laugh about that incident, but I ended up spending a lifetime trying to convince her that I was neither the "dummy" nor the prankster in that situation.

Bunkie and I did a lot of things in high numbers. So that moment of sharing with her was just one of billions that proved significant to my developing a sense of morality and human kindness. We also shared many other moments in a far more direct and perfect way. Until my eleventh grade year, most locations of school districts where Bunkie taught made it impossible for her to live at home on a daily basis. But without failure, she was home every Christmas and during the summer months. Whenever she was home, I was the taming target of parenting sessions; always by word (her lectures) and sometimes by deed (her whippings).

"Fuss-awhile, whip-awhile" was such a standard punishment for my friends and me during the prechild abuse and due process era that we secretly composed an eleventh commandment: "Thou shalt not whip us more than once a week." Since Bunkie was much more forgiving than forgetful, most of my whippings were for an accumulation of things I had done from the time of my birth. Between her many hits and misses, she recalled my ill-done deeds one by one. Hence, the older I got, the longer my whippings; they were even longer when she totally missed her aim.

One time, Bunkie was so "non–due-processed" that she actually began whipping me in error. Not only was she mistaken, she was guilty of the very act for which I was being whipped. She felt my pain and her guilt; later that day she baked and presented me my favorite chocolate cake.

In the two years following my tenth-grade year, I didn't have to wait on Christmas and summertime whippings. Bunkie was home every day.

Bunkie's disciplinary actions had an impact that was totally unexpected. Ironically, my unearned whipping of the century and other incidents that we laughed about through the years proved valuable to me in the more critical times of my mom's dementia. Whenever she was extremely irritable or disoriented, I engaged her in laughing about those incidents. That strategy worked even when all Bunkie could do was barely smile and say "yeah" to indicate that she remembered the incidents.

In all fairness about the whipping matter, my ego was hurt more than anything. My problem was being influenced by the notion that children, especially teenagers, are much older, wiser, and far more experienced than their parents. The worldwide term for that problem is "misbehavior by reason of peer stupidity."

Now that I am more "seniorized," I feel misbehavior among kids should be classified as the first order of dementia because it strays from the course of parental expectations.

Through it all, Bunkie remained an expert in bringing me all the way back to the realities of her world and power, and always accomplished that mission within a matter of minutes by her words and deeds. By the efforts of our parents, my friends and I lived to be healthy survivors of the pain and torture we caused ourselves at the hands of our parents. Each of us graduated from college and became God's gifts as professionals in education, law, government, and medicine. I even became an amateur tournament bowler; winning big bucks!

Later in time, I would realize that my mom was my greatest resource on life and my greatest example of how to live. At the outset of my adulthood, I relied more on Bunkie's wisdom. Even things she had said to me during my childhood, as she nurtured my personal growth and worth, had newer meaning and became more important. More and more, I actually began relating to her "lectures." I would also grow to understand why my mom was so effective whenever I went to her with concerns or critical decisions that I needed to make. No matter how long or how many times we discussed a particular matter, Bunkie always left me with the same advice, "Just put your trust in God. . . ."

Trusting in God was Bunkie's solution for every circumstance of life, especially involving grief, illness, fear, and controversy. She could be so compelling with that advice, whether the concern was mine, hers, or anybody else's. When President Bush issued the forty-eight-hour ultimatum for Saddam Hussein to leave Iraq or face military invasion, I could imagine Bunkie's reactionary demeanor. I could imagine her on the phone or in person with friends, discussing patiently their concerns, fears, and opinions about the threat of war and finally saying to whomever, "Just put your trust in God." Essentially, Bunkie's complete package of parenting was delivered to me by "word, deed, and faith."

Bunkie's faith in God was paramount to her regard

for life and the way in which she lived. She had an extensive record of active involvement in the Christian Methodist Episcopal church (CME). Her longest membership of fifty-three years at West Mitchell Street CME Church in Atlanta was her last. Bunkie rarely missed the Sunday morning worship service in her eighty-seven years, and had the distinction of being among the first few women in the CME Connection ever appointed to the Office of Steward at the local church level. True to her frequent claim, Bunkie had been "just about everything in the church except the preacher."

When her declining health was at its lowest ebb, Bunkie's awareness of, and faith in, God remained at a visible level. Her last birthday was May 31, 2000, less than five weeks before her death. As the two of us celebrated at home by her bedside, Bunkie uttered her favorite Bible verse in the way she often did when mocking a child's recitation that she had heard many years before, "The Lord is my Shepherd, and that's all I want!" Bunkie's involvement with God also seemed evident in our final moments together. Getting to those moments begins with her brief period of confinement.

We went for emergency medical service twice within two days because Bunkie stopped eating. She was hospitalized on the second trip. Little more than two weeks later, upon the advice and assistance of hospital personnel, Bunkie was transferred directly from the hospital to a nursing home. This placement was for several reasons.

Primarily, as Bunkie said to her doctors and visitors, she was not "sick sick." She just would not or could not eat. Once a feeding tube was installed, Bunkie no longer needed to be hospitalized, but needed full time health care that I was unable to provide, professionally, because I didn't have the necessary skills. Her insurance did not include coverage for the feeding tube, full-time care at home, or staying in a nursing home. But Medicaid would.

Bunkie had qualified several years for Medicaid, but never considered applying for that coverage. In view of the urgency of her situation and with my consent, the financial coordinator of the hospital proceeded to apply for Medicaid on Bunkie's behalf. That meant Bunkie's placement in the nursing home would be about eight weeks, after which I could bring her home.

There was no doubt in my mind that God was in motion. Medicaid was on the way! I gained a new sense of comfort. I no longer had to entertain the immediate options of Bunkie and me becoming homeless, my taking to the streets with a tin can to beg for alms, or going to jail for robbing a train in the spirit of Jesse James.

During the eighteen days of Bunkie's confinement between the nursing home and hospital, I visited her twice each day. My visits were always two hours, and much longer if she were awake. In addition to entangling ourselves in a gigantic hug, each visitation began and ended with my conducting a pop psychology session.

Bunkie, Jr. (while poking Bunkie, Sr. all over her body):
"Are you in any kind of pain? Are you sore anywhere?"
Bunkie, Sr. (with sparkling eyes and a broad smile):
"No."
Bunkie, Jr. (trying one more time, again and again, to lure Bunkie, Sr. into eating):
"Are you ready for a little something to eat?"
Bunkie, Sr. (still smiling with sparkling eyes):
"No, I'm not hungry just yet. I'll get something later."

Bunkie, Jr. (still trying, coaxing, tricking, cajoling, hoping, wishing, begging):

"Remember, as soon as you eat just a little bit, we can go home. Are you still ready to go home?"

Bunkie, Sr. (great big broad smile with eyes at a much brighter sparkling level, and trying to rally in a sit-up position):

"Yeah, I'm ready. Let's go home!"

Bunkie, Jr. (got it made this time around):

"Okay! So, do you want some food from your tray or some good old fried chicken and ice cream from home?"

Bunkie, Sr. (back to just smiling and plain sparkling eyes):

"No, honey, I'll eat later on. We going home now?"

Whenever Bunkie asked about going home, the pain of indicating that she could go if she were to eat never got easier. In fact, it became increasingly harder, especially at the end of our visits. I could fake my feelings better as we began our visits because I would go each time with the hope that she just might begin to eat again.

For several reasons, our visit on the eve of Bunkie's death was emotionally uplifting. After our "ceremonial" beginning, we talked and laughed more than we had in the last five or six days. She appeared more mentally alert, though her level of interaction had stabilized at two- to three-word sentences. However, as I prepared to leave her that evening, I began the are-you-ready-to-go-home ritual. For the first time in eighteen days, at the rate of twice per day (remember?), Bunkie said something that I never analyzed or really internalized until after her death. When I asked if she still wanted to go home, Bunkie responded with a most pleasant "No, no, no, no." She even responded with a rhythmic beat in her voice.

The surprise of her response caused me to repeat the question. In turn, Bunkie repeated her response in the same rhythmic tone of voice. We laughed and talked about her response. When I reminded her that Bandit and Whimper, our cats, were awaiting her return home, another "first" happened. Bunkie was totally noncommittal about seeing them. Though Bandit and Whimper were a major conversational piece for us, I dismissed her failure to respond.

About ten minutes later, I asked the same question. This time, she responded with her familiar prolonged nooooooooo, and was very happy while making her response. We eventually hugged and kissed good-bye. I threw her a kiss from the door, and she threw me one from her bed; I tarried at the door while she managed that effort. That was the last time I would see my mother alive.

In more pensive times, I reconciled Bunkie's death, believing that her persistence in saying no to coming home was due to a recent encounter that she had experienced with God. That encounter could have been in progress at the time of her response. I also interpreted the smile on her face as her way of telling me that she had seen God and was on her way to be with Him.

Two years later, while jotting down notes about Bunkie, I had a "senior" moment of my own. I went from the den to my bedroom for a most important reason that's no longer remembered. I didn't remember the reason as long as the few seconds it took for me to get to my bedroom. However, not to be outdone by my failed memory, I returned to sit where I had been sitting in the den; then I remembered.

So filled with happiness that my memory had retrieved itself, I simply laughed. I thought about Bunkie, and suddenly, the thought, "God happens," came to my mind and lingered a couple of days. That thought led to others, resulting in a poem that I wrote as a testament to my mom's faith in God and her influence on my relationship with God.

God Happens!

Before wakening to skies in royal array,
Ordained with the dawn of each new day,
God happens and opens my eyes!
He's my Creator who reigns in the sun.

And when I rise to earth's stage on my feet,
In the wintry cold or summer heat,
God happens and supplies my needs!
He's my Creator who loves me with care.

When in solitude or amidst a crowd,
I whisper or speak His name aloud,
God happens and hears my voice!
He's my Creator who abides with me.

When chosen pathways lead me astray
Because I fail His word to obey,
God happens and has mercy on me!
He's my Creator who saves me by grace.

When my climb in life is glorious and grand
Or I fall in need of a helping hand,
God happens and blesses me again!
He's my Creator who never fails.

When my spirit is broken in passionate grief,
And I seek His presence of calm relief,
God happens and strengthens me!
He's my Creator who comforts me with peace.

When birds perch my window, and sweetly sing
Or flutter to welcome the warmth of spring,
God happens and smiles with me!
He's my Creator who gives me joy.

When day has faded with the setting sun,
And my slumber, by night, once more begun,
God happens and watches over me!
He's my Creator who never leaves me alone.

Friendship, Strangers,
and an Elf of God

Bunkie's ties with the many genuine friends she made along the way lasted as long as she and her friends lived. Bunkie outlived most of those closest to her in age. Among her surviving friends is one of my personal and professional idols, Mrs. Ruth Reed. From the time we met, she became my "Aunt Ruth," and holds the title of being Bunkie's closest and dearest friend. The history of their friendship is a major chapter of Bunkie's life.

Bunkie began her college education at State Teachers and Agricultural College in Forsyth, Georgia. Bunkie and others commonly called the school "State Teachers College." She graduated in 1939 with the highest diploma awarded by that institution, which was the junior college diploma. That diploma was also the first of her professional teaching credentials. Her graduation year was the last year of operation for "her" State Teachers College. It was also the first year an institution in nearby Fort Valley, Georgia, operated under the university system of Georgia as The Fort Valley State College (FVSC), and remains a four-year institution with a graduate division.

Bunkie decided to begin the rest of her college work at FVSC the summer immediately following her graduation from State Teachers College. Upon arriving in Fort Valley, she was faced with one problem. All campus housing had been taken and Bunkie was left with nowhere to lay her head. Luckily, she came upon the campus handyman, "Dad" Mathis.

Everybody knew Dad Mathis, and Dad Mathis knew everything about the campus and town. He was the main fixer-upper, who had free range over all campus needs. He did everything from grooming the campus grounds to repairing leaks and distributing rolls of toilet paper upon request. Dad Mathis was such a responsible and responsive Johnny-on-the-spot person that students informally called him "president."

Dad Mathis proved quite helpful in Bunkie's search for summer housing. He referred her to Mrs. Hart, whose home was located directly across the street from the campus. Fortunately, Mrs. Hart accommodated Bunkie's need for a room that summer and did so for the remainder of the time Bunkie attended Fort Valley State. Mrs. Hart just happened to have been none other than Aunt Ruth's mother. And that's how Bunkie and Aunt Ruth were able to meet.

At the time Bunkie began rooming in Mrs. Hart's home, Aunt Ruth was teaching in Quitman, Georgia. Being a newlywed and working out of town, miles away from her husband, she preferred giving up her job. But there was one problem Aunt Ruth needed resolved.

Except for death and dying in that era and that region of public education, teacher resignation before the end of the school year was a cardinal sin. In some cases, teachers were able to break their contracts if somebody was on standby to fill the position. Aunt Ruth wanted a break from work, and Bunkie wanted a break from school. Bunkie put going to school on hold and was hired as a replacement in Aunt Ruth's position. Alternating between periods of working and going to school, Bunkie received the Bachelor of Science degree in August of 1947.

Eventually, Aunt Ruth, her husband (my "Uncle Reed"), and her mom lived together in Fort Valley. Through the years of friendship between our families, their home was ours and our home was theirs. Every time our families visited each other, eating a lot of food was a main event. When Bunkie and I visited in their home, Mrs. Hart, whom Bunkie and I affectionately called "Hartee" (Har tee), faithfully prepared my favorite breakfast dish. No matter the time of day, I was sure to have some of her delicious scrambled eggs and whatever else she had cooking.

The second event on the agenda was a significant on-going competition between Aunt Ruth and me. Bunkie and Hartee knew to expect being ignored. Aunt Ruth had taught me the game of Scrabble. After a few years of endless defeat, I finally won a game. Aunt Ruth's partial response to my triumph was, "The teacher hasn't taught until the student exceeds the teacher." Indeed, the teacher had taught!

Of my three main Scrabble buddies, Aunt Ruth is the most challenging player I ever encountered. Both of us are still progressive Scrabble addicts; when we play, we play long hours at a time. For years, I made solo trips to Fort Valley just to play Scrabble with Aunt Ruth. Although I managed a few more narrow wins over her, that first victory is one of the high points in my life.

Aunt Ruth also converted me to a nighthawk. Before her retirement, she was curriculum director of the Peach County School System in Georgia. Many times, I observed and admired the scholarly manner in which she did heavy-duty paper work in the wee hours of the night. So following her footsteps through my college years and graduate school, I waited until the wee hours of the night to begin studying. Even now, when I have a presentation to make, any written preparation is begun late in the night.

Aunt Ruth survived her husband and mother and lived alone about twenty years before moving to Knoxville, Tennessee, in the late 1990s. She resides there with her sister. During a subsequent phone conversation, Aunt Ruth asked a favor of me. I never said no, but I reluctantly said yes. Again, there was a problem, and the problem was me. Aunt Ruth and her sister were shortly on their way to Atlanta and were relying, as well they should have, on my home as a place to lay their heads. For weeks, with probable justification, my bedrooms and den had been in disarray with no hope of order before their arrival. Whereas I never said no, my slowly said yes probably had the tone effect of no. Much to my regret, Aunt Ruth did not make the trip. Her sister came, but stayed elsewhere. I also cut myself out of a long overdue Scrabble match with Aunt Ruth.

After that conversation, I knew instantly that had Bunkie been involved, her immediate response to Aunt Ruth's request would have been, "Why sure!" There would have been no hesitation, neither any forethought. In situations of that sort, my mother's nature was to consent first and, then, proceed to make a way out of any way. Rarely was there a time when Bunkie failed to accommodate the needs of others. If she could not handle a situation on her own, her next step was finding somebody who could. She seldom failed in that mission, because one of her primary skills was that of persuasion. She could, and would, wear anybody down to a yes point. No doubt, God gotta handful now!

As a child, I did not always take too kindly to

Bunkie's gestures of kindness. For instance, she knew of my obsessive passion for any kind of chocolate-anything. Yet, on too many occasions, seemingly every time we had a newly baked chocolate cake, she appeared to invite the whole neighborhood in for the sole purpose of devouring the cake. As I advanced in my childhood years, I began taking action to protect my interests. I went to the extreme at my birthday parties. I threatened my guests, telling them to eat ice cream only, as if a doctor had taken them off of chocolate cake. I was ever so grateful to outgrow the tradition of celebrating my birthday with greedy little friends.

Sometimes in her benevolent performance, Bunkie could be downright aggressive. She would become the only one who knew what was good for the goose and the gander. People who came to our home for any reason never left without the courtesy of being invited to stay for dinner, and any other meal. If they could not stay, Bunkie made sure they left with food items. If those who ate dinner were too full to eat dessert, Bunkie practically rammed it down their throats. We had a lot of big relatives and friends who enjoyed coming to our home, and they were never on a diet.

Bunkie enjoyed sharing everything, including me (my time, energy, and developing talents). Bunkie bought a typewriter for me when I was in college. I was a hunt-and-peck typist who typed only out of personal necessity. Typing was a chore for me because of my words-per-minute record. Therefore, I never enjoyed typing. But there was a lady (an elderly lady) who was a retired medical doctor that my mother had somehow befriended. During the few remaining years she lived, I typed more for her because my mother knew "somebody who could type."

The first year I started working, my mom helped me to buy my first automobile. Immediately thereafter, Bunkie transformed me into a human taxicab stand. Every Sunday when the church service was over, Bunkie recruited a line of our church members to join my grandmother and her in the car. Two of our frequent passengers lived at least twenty miles apart, and both of them lived at least twenty miles from our home. The remaining lucky rider lived nearer, but in an opposite direction, just as the other two lived in opposite directions from each other and our house.

I was Bunkie's personal transport service person from 1964 until 1968. The 1968–69 school year, I left home to work in Flint, Michigan. Upon returning home for Christmas break, my mother surprised me with a car of her own. My grandmother and I were very happy for Bunkie. For the next sixteen years, on Sundays after church, my grandmother and I dined together either at home or our favorite Piccadilly cafeteria. Bunkie joined us at home three to five hours later, after transporting her passengers home. With an increase of two more passengers, there was no telling how many miles she traveled per Sunday.

Family and friends were always Bunkie's top priority. But she also extended her kind and giving spirit beyond those she knew. Bunkie had a generous heart of love and compassion for all people. Her tendency, as well as her delight, was assuming responsibility for the comfort and needs of others, whether known or unknown.

Greeting strangers was a formal art for Bunkie. In fact, she added new meaning to Webster's definition of "stranger." Whether Bunkie was in a store or bank, at church, on the telephone, or wherever, she was a welcome wagon all by herself. Her main venue for talking to strangers was any kind of store, while I stood or sat in waiting for her.

Life as a stranger in my mother's presence lasted no longer than the time needed for the stranger and Bunkie to exchange names. After that point, Bunkie extracted the person's whole life history in her famous inquisition. She obtained extensive data on the person's residential status and place of birth, marital and employment status, number of children and their vital statistics, church membership, number of siblings and their place of residence, origin of parents and their whereabouts, educational background, and much more.

One day, Bunkie went to pick up a visiting friend from the now extinct Atlanta Terminal train station. This was in the early sixties. In the process of waiting for the train to arrive, she began talking with a stranger, a young adult female. For whatever reasons, the young lady was stranded in the train station and would not be able to leave Atlanta before early the next morning. Upon learning that this stranger was a freshman at Fort Valley State, my mother brought her into our home, fed her, and bedded her for the night.

The next morning, after breakfast and at Bunkie's persistence, the young lady dressed up in my never-had-a-chance-to-wear brand new pair of pants. The price tag was still attached. She left with the solemn promise of returning my pants to me. We never saw her or the pants again.

On another occasion, Bunkie had been on the phone almost half an hour. She was having so much fun that I interrupted to find out who had called. We often butted in each other's calls for that purpose and to correct or offer personal opinions to the conversation in progress. Inasmuch as I did not recognize the name Bunkie gave, I left them to their conversation. The two of them continued to talk longer than another whole hour. At one point, I know a mutual friend was discussed. From all indications, both of them had known this friend for years.

When the conversation ended, Bunkie told me that she enjoyed talking to the lady, but did not know her. The lady had not only dialed the wrong number, she had reached Bunkie, the interrogator.

Varying circumstances altered Bunkie's inquisition only twice, to my knowledge. On her first appointment with a doctor to whom she had been referred, the doctor beat Bunkie at her own game. After answering questions number one, two and three, the doctor revealed the rest of his life story on his own, and nonstop. Just as Bunkie was about to be led away and prepped for her physical exam, the doctor asked me, "Is your mother always like this?" With a sheepish grin I responded, "You ain't seen nothing yet!" The doctor continued to be amused and in awe of Bunkie's personality for the duration of the appointment. As we left the doctor's office, I could not resist saying to him that Bunkie was the current director of the FBI. Naturally, he laughed while confirming the same. He also indicated for Bunkie to call him if she had need to do so. Bunkie thanked him and responded, "And you be sure to call me if you need me."

The second situation was a matter of preventing me from getting a traffic ticket, or worse. We were traveling through a town where Bunkie and her stepfather had old ties. My grandmother, who was in the car at the time, also had familiarity in the town. The minute the policeman pulled us over, Bunkie took charge. She changed her inquisitive routine and engaged the policeman in talking about her then-deceased stepfather and other people she had known to live in the town. When she finally finished, the policeman allowed us to go on our way with a smile and no ticket. The ticket he issued before stopping us was probably his last ticket for that day.

Perhaps the most stunning of Bunkie's interviews with strangers occurred December of 1999. I summoned an ambulance because Bunkie had suddenly slipped into an unconscious state. The paramedics arrived quickly and found Bunkie's vital signs to be extremely faint. They worked to revive her for several minutes before placing her in the ambulance. Their effort was continued in the ambulance for several more minutes before leaving for the hospital. Initially, the indicator screen inside the ambulance showed no activity of life. I imagine that at that time Bunkie and God were taking care of some real serious business.

The minute my mother regained consciousness, she asked the attendants their names and just a few more questions. She was brief in that session because the attendants, with a little difficulty, cautioned her against exerting herself. In response to their caution, Bunkie smiled and said, "I feel fine as wine." And on to the hospital we merrily went. The ambulance driver never knew that he was transporting a dignitary in the person of a non-appointed FBI director.

The only people never subjected to Bunkie's thousand questions were the sick and homeless. One Christmas during the mid-nineties, we went to visit a church member in the nursing home. The walls were beautifully decorated for the season. Bunkie and I were especially attracted to a display of Santa and his elves. As we continued to stroll through the home that evening, Bunkie slowed her gait and stopped at intervals just to look at the decorations. Every now and then, I took her by the hand and said, "Come on little elf of God."

The staff and residents in the nursing homes where we went more frequently looked forward to our coming. This was especially true among those whom we had "taken under our wings." As we greeted different ones while walking to our destination, we stopped and talked with them about their day and other things. Bunkie always gave them peppermints and left them smiling with the assurance that we would see them again real soon. A few of the residents, unable to remember Bunkie's earthly departure, continued to ask, "Where is your mother?"

Bunkie's generous regard for the poor and homeless was of no less quality. There were a couple of beggars whose presence we looked for when in certain areas of Atlanta. Bunkie often gave them what she called "a little taste of change." Bunkie's idea of the poor, however, extended beyond the homeless, financially disabled, hungry, or those in need of clothes. Her poor included all social rejects, the weak in mind, and those broken in spirit.

One of our church members, by her own admission, was diagnosed as being manic-depressive. After her husband's death, she developed a closer relationship with Bunkie and me. She became more dependent on us for personal assistance and emotional support. For little more than five years, Bunkie availed herself to this member any time she needed or just wanted to talk. The two of them talked by phone every day, conversing many times more than once a day. Their standard ritual was reciting the Twenty-third Psalm and praying the Lord's Prayer every night, even if one of them was out of town.

Eugene Patterson, a former editor of *The Atlanta Constitution,* once wrote in his column, "Somewhere the poor must live." Bunkie agreed and was even more committed to the position that the poor, by her standards, are also entitled to human dignity. She did her best, as an "elf of God," to make her position a reality of life.

Behavior Is Learned, but Personality Is Born

Human behavior has been the target of scientific research for centuries. Among the participants is a large number of dogs, monkeys, and other animals whose lives were spent proving that human beings do not really choose a personality. Until proven otherwise, ancient and modern-day behavioral theorists agree that human behavior is the output of hereditary and environmental factors that, in turn, shape the human personality. Our personality is what we are and do. Hence, we are what we do and we do what we are.

Somehow, Bunkie matured with more of a *born* personality. Her strong sense of purpose, security, and self-will was definitely not a gift from the neighborhood. In fact, nobody just happens to become the kind of person Bunkie was without being born that way.

Yes, No, Maybe So

Bunkie never thought of herself as being better than anybody, but she was in a few areas. For instance, a number of people would join me in citing Bunkie as one of the most carefree individuals that ever lived. Worrying was not a visible part of her personal agenda. Therefore, she never would have qualified for a worrying contest. Whenever Bunkie encountered a rough road in life, she did what she could to smooth it out, if possible. Otherwise, she presented the matter to God in prayer and moved onward.

Though she sincerely cared about people, Bunkie was an unassuming person who cared very little about what others assumed, believed, or thought. In matters of trivia or lacking in facts or common sense, her already unassuming disposition was far more activated. If somebody believed salt was pepper or the earth was a purple nine-sided triangle, Bunkie left that person to his or her convictions. She was a firm believer in the principle of self-discovery and never flaunted the truth by saying, "I told you so."

Another feature of her carefree nature was an enduring noncommittal and evasive attitude. There were times when she operated in her unassuming, noncommittal, or evasive mode when I referred to her as my "roommate." She also adopted that reference, the significance of which originated during my college days.

One of the greatest thrills of being a residential college student is breaking rules without getting caught. All rules that created personal inconveniences were the first to be broken by my generation of residential students. At my alma mater, which is also FVSC, one of the broadest written, best remembered, and most frequently violated laws of the land forbade ironing in dormitory rooms. A huge, clean, and well-lit area was reserved in the basement of each dorm for that chore.

With the exceptions of going to class, to a game or sock-hop, or to the dining hall, walking up and down flights of stairs was a classified inconvenience. The absence of elevators in the dorms, therefore, justified our purpose in life. Residential students were born to break dormitory policies.

Dormitory matrons had the inherent authority to conduct unannounced room checks, and did so about once a week. One morning, my roommate was caught red-handed. Not only was she ironing. She was using an ironing board that had been "slightly borrowed" from the basement.

Our saintly and respected matron, stunned in her tracks, said to my roommate, "Young lady, are you ironing?"

My roommate continued ironing and replied politely, "No, ma'am!"

Showing great evidence of being baffled, the matron said, "I see," and left.

She was too dumbfounded to impose a penalty and never knew how really scared my roommate was by the thought of being possibly suspended.

As an innocent and speechless spectator, I thought the episode was absolutely priceless. Their reaction to each other presented an almost perfect impasse of "dual evasion." Only my mother's involvement could have provided the height of total perfection. Bunkie thrived off of responding, in kind, to anybody who dared ask about anything that was already "self-evident."

In some cases, a lot of creativity was needed to either predict or prepare for my mom's intentions and related actions. I had to use all of my brain cells many times when she needed or wanted me to do something for her. She generally gave me advanced notice of her plans. But such notification from Bunkie seldom served any purpose beyond being a matter of courtesy.

Whether she served notice a month or minutes ahead, on the day of her intended activity, I always had to reconfirm her plans. That effort was another matter of futility in my life. But it was also a matter of protocol and necessary for the sake of peace, harmony, and understanding. She rarely indicated a change in plans, verbally, that is. After allowing several hours of the day to pass, I would question her intentions for the last time. That final confirmation was not only sought as a courtesy. It was sought to determine whether I should proceed with any personal plans I may have made for the same day.

If her plans included going somewhere, she always gave one of two responses, if not both: "Yes, I guess I'll still go" or "Yeah, I'm ready. I just need to do a little something." Sometimes, she would be ready, but never moved toward the door between our kitchen and carport. About half a year after I began driving, I learned to never make personal plans on or for any day that Bunkie intended to involve me in her plans.

When operating under those circumstances, or any others, getting a direct answer from my mother was next to impossible and a rare occurrence. Columbus discovered America with much less effort and in less time. Bunkie's response about her plans to do anything was essentially the same under any circumstance. Whether dressed to go or still clad in pajamas, her response meant either yes, no, or maybe so, and would be my only automatic clue to "wait and see." But the moment she asked whether we had enough time to carry out her plans, I knew she would eventually cancel them. That was only one of her indirect ways of saying "no."

By virtue of her nature, being noncommittal and evasive was one of my mother's greatest areas of mastery. She made "creative prediction" a way of life for most people who knew her ways. The better she knew a person, the more likely that person was to be duped by her unassuming, noncommittal, and evasive charm and wit. Including her former students, the number of her victims probably reached well into the high thousands.

Time Is Not an Issue, It's a Fortune

In conjunction with universal design, man was not destined to live by bread alone. In addition to the air we breathe, water we drink, and money we spend, we must have time to do things. Some of us have a little bit more time than others, but Bunkie was an extremist. She had more time than anybody and deliberately took her time doing just about everything. Bunkie took her time rushing. I doubt very seriously that her abundance of time had anything to do with her managerial or organizational skills. The only explanation may be amusing, but totally unbelievable.

Shortly after Bunkie's birth, the element of time was broken into portions and distributed to all the little newborn babies on a "first come, first get all you want" basis. Bunkie just happened to have been first in line and reaped a fortune.

Returning to the truth of her nature, time was never an issue for Bunkie. Time was her self-made fortune in life. She consistently gave unlimited time to her top priorities, which remained three throughout her life. God and family were the first two, and in that order. Church and friends tied for third. Her job came in fifth place because of the tie for third.

Except for getting to church and work on time, keeping an isolated promise, and responding to emergencies requiring haste, time was not a crucial matter to Bunkie.

After a few experiences of waiting longer than an hour for her to pick me up from the airport, I changed my scheduled arrival to an hour earlier. The longest we waited on the other thereafter was less than fifteen minutes. Bunkie never scheduled time. She just consumed it and always had some to spare.

Bunkie's most prominent use of time was for talking. Conversing with others was her main forte and a hobby that she enjoyed to the nth degree. The telephone was invented to maximize that pleasure in her life. Bunkie caused telemarketers to lose their sense of purpose when they called.

Bunkie would talk and listen to anybody, regardless of race, color, creed, sex, origin, size, economic status, I.Q., or species. We had as many as six cats at one time, and she talked to them a lot. The cats were not mentioned previously as top priority because they were our family members.

More than twenty of the last twenty-two years of her life, Bunkie was often the last person to exit from our Sunday morning worship service. Several times, I managed to cut the lights off in the sanctuary to free her captive audience of one to two people. My next hurdle was leaving the parking lot. Within any given hour, Bunkie and her cotalkers said the word "good-bye" five to ten times before it meant anything. I lost a lot of gas switching the motor on and off. The result was the same whether we were together in the car on a parking lot or in a friend's driveway.

I often invited Bunkie to accompany me to personal engagements. Most of them were banquets or other formal programs that I either coordinated or on which I was a guest participant. In addition to having a good time, Bunkie's key role was to serve as my critic. My only regrets at the end of each affair were not knowing where the main light switch was located and having to buy gas the next day.

Bunkie achieved posthumous fame among her fellow chatterers for the one-liner she used in ending conversations. If the conversation was by phone, she seldom hung up before saying, "Well, you call me again 'cause we got to talk!" In person, her ending was modified: "Remember now, we got to talk!"

Another great percentage of Bunkie's time was used for shopping. Long periods of my life as a child were spent sitting in the shoe shop of one of our major downtown department stores while Mama and Bunkie shopped. The workers in the shoe shop seemed to expect me on Saturdays. I almost had a reserved seat. Unfortunately for me, the department store was surrounded by other different kinds of stores. When Mama and Bunkie shopped in those other stores, my sitting time increased as their designated bag keeper.

Whenever Mama finished shopping, usually within three hours, the two of us ate in the department store's cafeteria. After eating, we returned to the shoe shop and sighed in restlessness while waiting about three more hours for Bunkie.

My childhood periods of time deprivation ended when I was old enough to stay at home alone. Eventually, I was also old enough to choose between going and not going to shop. In the best interest of my time, I chose to take extensive periods of personal leave from Mama and Bunkie's all-day shopping expeditions. The less often I went shopping, the less often my ever-growing and strong dislike for shopping was displayed.

In all fairness, shopping with Mama was a pleasure because she understood the process of shopping and went about it in a timely fashion. Rarely did we need more than two hours to shop, and once the two of us finished, we dined before going home.

Bunkie, on the other hand, violated the entire concept of shopping because time was "her fortune." She was born to monopolize her time and some of what others managed to scrape from other planets. By the time Bunkie finished shopping, I just wanted to go home.

Shopping with Bunkie just to get our cats some chow, canned meat, and milk was a hassle. One day, we managed to get in and out of the store within a half hour; it was bona fide freedom!

To Buy or Not to Buy

I gradually resumed shopping with Bunkie, but not often, because of a major discovery I made. Bunkie prolonged her shopping time by taking twenty minutes or longer deciding on one item. That was her habit in any kind of store, and a total of eight items was her bare minimum. Shoe store clerks didn't stand a chance with Bunkie.

Sometimes, after taking a long time inspecting an item, her final decision was to check on it at another store on that same day or buy it another day. A few times she waited until the next year. There were also many times when she inspected several of the same items at the rate of ten minutes each, only to buy the item she first inspected. Naturally, she had to inspect that same item again. The last ten minutes were definitely the longest.

Store clerks were always very generous in their patience with my mom, and many of them took great pride in waiting on her. Their patience, however, led Bunkie to conclude that the clerks had just as much time as she had. Encouraged by their attentiveness, she never realized the strain of her monopoly on time. In addition to the store clerk's time, Bunkie monopolized the time of customers waiting to be waited on. The customers probably waited out of curiosity just to find out how long Bunkie would take. The whole truth is that Bunkie was just a plain delightfully slow person. The possibility is quite high that whenever she finished her shopping, the store clerks and customers just wanted to go home too!

By the time I was eighteen, our procedures for shopping together were changed in the interest of protecting my emotional stability. Once inside a store, we agreed on a "sitting" area to meet after completing our shopping. The purpose of that agreement was achieved with one exception. Every now and then, Bunkie would meet me and leave me to either buy or check on one more item. As soon as I got my first car, I waited on Bunkie in the car. Pending the nature of our shopping spree, I even gave Bunkie a two-hour head start before I went into the store. I still ended up waiting on her in the car.

The year of 1968 was, indeed, a very good year. Happiness that year and for the next twenty-nine years was Bunkie having a driver's license and a car of her own. Owning a car, however, leads to changing cars, and changing cars means buying cars. Buying a car means going shopping. Unfortunately, when Bunkie shopped for a car, the happiness that came with her owning a car died in the minutes, hours, days, weeks, and even months of time consumption.

Once Bunkie selected a car, the actual transaction of the deal took her anywhere between a week and two months. But once she signed the dotted line, a sound of jubilation could be heard throughout the dealership. The longest and shortest time Bunkie took to make a final decision about buying a car occurred the same year, four months apart.

The two of us shopped for our cars together on three occasions, and dealt with the same salesman each time. The last time we went car-shopping together was in 1987. Bunkie was her normal unassuming, noncommittal, and evasive self. However, her performance was a pure mockery of a notable Shakespearean scene. She played her to-buy-or-not-to-buy game to perfection, and the salesman fell for her antics all the while.

Learning nothing from previous deals with my mom, the salesman mistakenly assumed that Bunkie had settled on a car choice. He was so *wrong!* Operating on his assumption, he tagged the car for reserved status and contacted my mother at intervals for her final decision. He finally gave up about three weeks later.

The next month, I returned to the dealership to take care of some details regarding my new car. Bunkie was with me. Our salesman, in greeting my mom, assumed (*again*) that Bunkie was really ready to buy a car, because she seemed attracted to one particular car. Just like the car that struck her attention on our first visit, this car was loaded with a lot of stuff that Bunkie didn't want. The salesman, bless his heart, wrote a requisition for that car to be customized to accommodate my mother's preferences. That was a dreadful mistake! Bunkie never requested the car to be altered. Neither did she directly indicate an intention to buy the car. She simply inspected that particular car longer than she did the others.

The only known fact at hand was Bunkie's interest in buying a car. Her exact car choice and purchase date remained unknown. At the salesman's persistence, Bunkie returned to the dealership and examined the car that had been altered for her. The salesman felt from Bunkie's mere arrival that her buying time was nigh. In turn, he was more hopeful and convinced than ever. Their negotiations, however, proved to be no more than a bout of wasted time between her indecision and his determination.

Before we left, the salesman took one more risky step to please Bunkie, but with her consent. He ordered a car for her all the way from Michigan. The car was due to arrive about two weeks later.

When Bunkie got the call informing her that the car was ready for pickup, the history of her personality repeated itself. She told the salesman that she would "wait until another time" to buy a car. Hence, the ring decision for *indecision versus determination* was a "K.O." *Indecision* won the match by a landslide!

A little more than four months had passed between our initial shopping visit and the arrival of the car from Michigan. About a week or so after Bunkie and the salesman's last conversation, she and I went to a shopping mall. Bunkie went along just for the ride and remained in the car. Very shortly after leaving the mall, we spotted a new car dealership. Out of curiosity, we stopped for a casual visit to the showroom. Without any plans or hesitation, Bunkie purchased a car that day. We got home long before dark.

Bunkie's new car was a duplicate of the car she first considered at the other dealership. The year, make, model, and color were the same as mine. Her monthly payment, however, was $82.34 less than mine for the same number of years. That was not surprising, because her notes were less than mine the two previous times when we bought cars that were alike. One factor making the difference could have been the trade-in value based on our mileage, with my mileage usually four times greater.

It is more realistic, however, that each salesman, out of pure frustrated love and respect for my mom, asked Bunkie how much would she pay a month and agreed to her terms. The more I think about it, that explanation bears a lot of truth. Totally unlike my standard equipped cars, Bunkie's cars were always fully loaded with all the stuff that she didn't want and never used. Her last car purchase was made without my presence in 1992.

Each of us is destined to be wealthy in some of kind of way, some people in more ways than others. Bunkie was wealthy in time, among several other things. The more time she invested, the more time she had. In her natural unassuming, noncommittal, and evasive ways, she spent most of her time living the life she loved and loving the life she lived. Time was Bunkie's life, and taking time was her personality. She was born that way.

Notable Reflections of Change and Circumstance

Time has a way of sifting the years of our lives and bringing forth memories from the smallest and most remote corner of our minds. Upon reaching the mind's mirrored surface, each memory reflects its own emotional value and weight; it becomes the joy or regret of remembering sensations of past situations as if they just happened the day before. Memories are also a source of maturation; we learn to never lay hands on a hot stove.

The older some memories become, the more precious they become, while others that we may or may not cherish retain their natural order. Some memories are modified to the extent that related perspectives lose their merit and the element of willful control, thereby causing us to change our minds.

One's right to a change of heart or mind may not be a civil declaration, but change is a universal way of life. At any time, the value or weight of a single memory can shift according to our experiences with people, places, and things. When shifts in our memory bank create change in our attitudes, perceptions, and actions, new memories are made and stored, one at a time. But the root of the original memory is never forgotten.

Never Means Never until It Happens

My lifetime with Bunkie left so much for me to re-member that I established a daily twenty-four-hour re-pository in my mind that bears her name as "Bunkie's archives." One of the earliest memories filed on her as my pioneer in life begins with my desire, intention, and promise to never attend her alma mater; it was a "town thing."

For a long time, the town of Fort Valley was purely a breeding ground for gnats, and all of the air consumed in breathing was filled with the odor of another town's ob-noxious pulp factory fumes from sunrise to almost sunset. The offensive smell was reason enough to not attend any-thing in Fort Valley. But I had other reasons more so-cially appropriate and far more beneficial to my athletic nature.

In the early spring of each year, college-bound se-niors at my high school participated in field trips to local minority colleges. A large number of seniors in the class immediately preceding my graduation year enrolled in the same college. Many of my classmates enrolled in two other local colleges, nationally recognized as brother-sis-ter institutions. Our goal was to be different from the pre-vious graduating class by not going where they went. My personal reason for "going with the flow" was even more nonacademic.

Initially, my firm decision was to attend the first col-lege we visited because I liked everything about the cafe-teria. It was a newly built and huge facility, and the lunch we were served was just plain down good! But the excite-ment of seeing a full-length swimming pool and a spa-cious well-kept tennis court led me to actually join the sisterhood at the second college we visited. I had been swimming and playing tennis for several years before going to college. Beginning with the first day of class, I refined the concept of Thomas Jefferson's "pursuit of happiness."

Bunkie had never attempted to influence my college choice and was quite happy with my decision. Fulfilling my mission of playing tennis and swimming for long hours on a daily basis, I lost my academic scholarship at the end of my very first semester of enrollment. My poor grades ultimately landed me on academic suspension at the end of my junior year, but with the possibility of readmission the second semester of the next school year.

As my mom reviewed my grades, I did my best to explain to her that most of my teachers were boring, and they really were. Several of them were old and boring. All of the proof was in the A's that I earned from those teachers who inspired me, some of whom were old. In addition to earning nine A's over those six semesters (and out of a total of thirty-six grades), I was the proud recipient of a senior lifeguard certificate and the lead participant in a local swimming exhibition. Six of my A's were in physical education. Of less significance, I played a lot of tennis with one of my favorite professors when I was supposed to be in some boring professor's class.

Everybody gets a second chance at something in life, and so it was with my college career. Without much discussion before, during or after what would become my last whipping in life, Bunkie paved the way for me to enroll at The Fort Valley State College the summer immediately following my junior year. Within one hour or less, I discovered that gnats and obnoxious odors can be easily ignored and forgotten.

Due to the learning and social environment and my personal adjustment at FVSC, I chose to complete my college experience there. About midway the school year, I dared pull a prank on my mom and grandmother, pretending to have been ejected from FVSC. At the time, I was in Atlanta to cover a Peace Corps conference as one of the editors of *The Peachite,* our school newspaper. Graduating a year off schedule, but with a reputable grade point average, I returned to FVSC the next year on full scholarship to pursue a master's degree. I never lost another scholarship.

I determined from my mom and grandmother's reaction that I had made them proud. I felt a strong sense of pardon and pride; all because I went where I *never* intended or wanted to go. Incidentally, FVSC had a full-length swimming pool, in which I never swam. And it is absolutely amazing what thirty years of urban development can do for the life of a town. You ought to see Fort Valley now!

From a professional perspective, my calling was to be a nurse, astronomer, tennis player, or a decorated officer in the United States Navy. Had I begun bowling before going to college, I would have retired as a professional bowler. I had considered several other realistic careers, none of which related to the professional field of education, let alone that of an elementary school teacher. That was Bunkie's calling and she was very good at what she did. But being an unofficial student in her class one summer was an unfortunate "never wanna do again" experience for me.

I was barely six years old at the time, and her class was a mixture of second-, third-, and fourth-grade students. I had fun participating in classroom activities and playing with them, but Bunkie also punished me with them, though I never participated in their crimes.

By the time I was ten years old, I definitely knew that

I would never be an elementary school teacher, because of Bunkie. She was forever drawing, coloring, and cutting out letters and creating stuff for her classroom bulletin boards and activities or school plays. Occasionally, Bunkie lured me into joining her efforts, fully knowing that I was an outdoor child who had not even engaged much in cutting out paper dolls. Once I passed the hide-and-seek stage, bicycle riding and skating were my top playtime activities. Helping Bunkie to mess up and clean up our mess of paper scraps and other litter limited my outdoor physical development time with the neighborhood kids. Half an hour makes a lot of difference in the pleasure of a child's life. That limitation made me commit to memory why I should never become an elementary school teacher.

When I initially began attending FVSC, most of my close friends there were majoring in various teaching fields. I just wanted to graduate. For whatever reasons, however, I took on a double minor, which included secondary education. At least I would not be bogged down with cutting, coloring, and pasting a whole lot of stuff every other day.

My first job was as a part-time high school guidance counselor in a small town just out of Atlanta. I also taught two classes. My one and only goal, however, was to work in the Atlanta Public School System (APS), but openings were scarce. Beginning teachers from miles around always sought employment in Atlanta. At the end of my first work year, taking my mother's advice, I opted to go exactly one-hundred miles that summer and enroll, *again,* at FVSC to satisfy requirements for state certification as an elementary school teacher. The intention was to increase my chances for employment with APS.

That opportunity came abruptly during the next

school year in December because of a new school scheduled to open after Christmas break. Of all the different kinds of schools in the world, it was an elementary school. I accepted the position, knowing that I could request a transfer to the high school level for the next year. Instead of pursuing a transfer, I spent the summer modifying my attitude about elementary school teaching. After all, I had sixth- and seventh-grade students, which wasn't such a terrible situation.

By choice, I remained at that school for two more years, and created one of the best memorable experiences of my professional career. Three years later, I did become a full time high school guidance counselor in Atlanta Public Schools. My professional resumé includes a variety of local, state, and national involvement and recognition all because of Bunkie and my change of heart. *Never*, indeed, prevailed until I did it!

The Working of a Master Plan

Reversal of the "never to be, do, or go" syndrome is not always initiated by a change of mind. Every now and then, as victims of circumstance, people are submissive because they are either weak and just can't help themselves or have no line of authority in the matter at hand. Bunkie and I shared a twenty-one-year experience of the sort that originated in an attempt to protect a specific area of our residential grounds.

Mama maintained a vegetable garden on and off for a great number of years. She planted her last garden in 1979, fully aware of the risks involved. Unfortunately, in addition to the potential of being damaged by weather conditions, gardens are main attractions for wildlife.

While in the planting stage of her garden, Mama decided on a master plan to prevent wildlife tampering with premature growth in the garden plot. The gardening terminology for wildlife tampering is "theft by nibbling and hole formation." Besides the birds that pecked the bounty of our fig tree, the leading culprits were chipmunks, rabbits, and squirrels.

The plan of action was not altogether a new thought. Mama had considered the same plan for protecting previous gardens, but that particular time she meant business! So, off she went to our former neighborhood and returned later with "the plan" bedded down on a towel in a box. The plan was a newborn kitten, packed with a miniature milk bottle.

Realizing that several weeks to four months would pass before her new recruit would be able to perform any task of outdoor protection, Mama secured a second kitten the next week. This feline recruit was about five months old, and would be ready for duty by the time any visible growth occurred in the garden.

Mama was very confident, proud, and secure as she awaited the time to activate her plan. *Never came!* Once the kittens came inside our home, they established their territories and trained themselves to request time-outs for biophysiological relief. They always extended their time outside to chase each other in play, but not the wildlife.

The newly born was a calico, which I named "Peep" because a black patch of hair surrounded one of her eyes. The second cat, an orange tabby identical to the befamed Morris the Cat, I named "Star."

Peep and Star represented a brand new experience for me, but Mama and Bunkie had dealt with transient cats and dogs during their life on Mama's residential farm. The "never" aspect associated with this experience was twofold. I never wanted another pet after our parakeet died in my tenth-grade year, and Mama and Bunkie had a lifetime standard that forbade cats and dogs in the house because of their nature to shed hair everywhere. That scenario, however, was changed drastically.

I developed an unconditional love for Peep and Star, and they grew up as my pets. Mama's plan of protection dwindled into defeat when Bunkie became more obvious in her attachment to Peep and Star. They were soon "our" household pets, but chose only the foot of my bed for their bed.

Within almost a year of the kittens' arrival in our home, Bunkie and I prepared a maternity station for Peep, who delivered a litter of four. In the absence of any planned parenthood effort by Peep, Mama and Bunkie knew and agreed that housing six cats would never work. So neither of us thought twice about giving the entire litter away. We thought only once and kept the entire litter. In the order of their births, they were named Alpha, Deuce, PJ (for Peep, Jr.), and Whimper. Peep and her daughters, Alpha, PJ, and Whimper, were spayed in a hurry!

Along with the joy they added to our lives came our shared pain of losing them, beginning with Peep and Alpha who died suddenly a year apart. Bunkie held graveside services for both on our front lawn. Star and Deuce disappeared in the snow a year apart. PJ and Whimper died of natural causes at the human age of 21 and 22, respectively. Their handsome adopted mixed calico brother invaded our home on his own as a baby kitten in 1988. His name is Bandit, and he never strays from our grounds. Unlike Star and Deuce, Bandit was "fixed" at an early age. In the words of the TV game show host, Bob Barker, "Please have your pets spayed or neutered."

The Longest Memory Is a Lasting Impression

If I were tested on my first impression of Bunkie, I would be sure to flunk for obvious reasons. First, of all, I was a baby when I had my first impression about anything. Secondly, at the time, I had no idea that my first impressions were expected to last the rest of my lifetime. Therefore, the age-old adage implying that "first impressions are lasting impressions" should be amended with a statute of limitations to exclude all impressions a person has before the age of two, with the exception of baby geniuses.

My lapse of recall from babyhood years, however, does not mean that Bunkie archives are void of lasting impressions. There are so many that a number needs to be created for reporting the total count. Regardless of the count, the search in my memory bank on Bunkie reveals that the majority of my greatest and longest lasting impressions relate to her parental role of support.

People do well to have an encouraging person around for the significant long haul in life; for the good times and bad, the thick and thin, and the ups and downs. I am not sure that I ever experienced the bad of life; but Bunkie was always there for my thin and down loads. It was one of the good times in my life that lacked her support; my twenty-year on-and-off again affair with the man I married.

Anybody who agrees with everything somebody does or says is totally un-American. Since Bunkie was a full-blooded American, I reconciled to welcoming her tolerance of my love affair.

Aside from that one void of support in my life, somewhere in the shadow of all my other endeavors, Bunkie was always there to encourage my success. For another long period of my life, twenty-two years to be exact, Bunkie was my personal cheerleader, though she never understood the mechanics of what I was doing. Those years were times she spent encouraging and complimenting my bowling activities and achievements.

Bunkie looked forward to accompanying me to bowling tournaments to watch me bowl. No matter what I did when it was my turn at the lane, Bunkie thought I was magnificent. She never recognized that it is not a good thing for any bowler to face the dreaded and mostly impossible-to-spare seven–ten split; especially when it happens twice in the same game. *Neither does one cheer!* Though I seldom left that particular split, whenever I did and knocked down one of the pins, Bunkie thought I was even more magnificent.

As each tournament shift ended, Bunkie usually asked, "Well, how did you do that time?" That was her way of finding out if my plan was to bowl the next shift. My routine was to re-enter until I was reasonably sure of placing "high in the money." Bunkie always encouraged me to stay as long as I needed and not be concerned about getting her home. Whatever my final place was in the tournament, Bunkie was happy; her classic response was, "I knew you could do it!"

I never doubted Bunkie's sincerity when she complimented my bowling, but her reviews and compliments were more meaningful to me when she had a greater understanding of the situation involved. In fact, my speaking engagements that she attended were not complete until she gave me her full assessment.

The tone of her soft or raised voice was the real indicator of how she felt about all things, with or without understanding. I usually knew when I had done well enough to earn the familiar tone of her voice as she softly exclaimed, "Bunkie, you did it!" Hearing those words from her was the height of my fulfillment. Anything she said short of that gratifying exclamation meant that my performance was no more than just "good." Her ratings were always accurate. Occasionally, my speeches were no better than just good.

Whether my involvements were significant or insignificant, Bunkie was equally encouraging. Anytime I played solitaire in her presence, she had an interest in whether I was winning. If I weren't, she responded, "You will because you're Carrie Grove's daughter!" The mention of our kinship was an old standard reference coined by one of our former physicians, the late Dr. Louis C. Brown.

Bunkie understood the complexity of the solitaire game I played about as much as she did the mechanics of bowling and the seven–ten split.

Encouragement was just one of my mom's longest suits. Bunkie was a prime example of a person leading three lives. She was an excellent daughter and parent, and an effortless 5 foot 9 1/2 inches human mass of secrets and tricks.

On one occasion, while talking to Bunkie from Missouri, I asked her to give me some information from a folder in my bedroom. After giving her the exact location of the folder, she made a priority out of the telephone bill and insisted on calling me back once she found the folder. Since our telephone bill was my responsibility, I cared less about the expense. So, winning the battle of insistence, I waited on the phone for her to find the folder.

About ten minutes later, Bunkie returned to the phone and told me that she was unable to find the folder, but would continue looking for it. Much later that night, still unable to find the folder, Bunkie called and asked if there were anywhere else from which to get the information I wanted. *Nowhere! No way!* The information I wanted was a written creation produced by my brain. Besides, getting it was not a matter of urgency.

A week later, Bunkie miraculously found the folder in the exact spot previously indicated, but a wee bit too late for my use.

I talked with Bunkie and Mama about five more times before returning home the next month for Thanksgiving. Hours after getting home, I was informed that while Bunkie was supposedly searching for the folder, she was in the hospital—neither as a visitor nor doctor. She was a patient whose extent of medical practice was home remedies. That's probably how she ended up being a patient.

Long distance calls between us several times a week were common. But Bunkie had called me five times from her hospital room within that particular week, hoping that I would not have reason to call home. Each time she called, Mama was "asleep," so Bunkie said. She feared Mama would snitch on her. But for a change, Mama supported Bunkie's game plan.

According to Bunkie, her reason for being hospitalized was "nothing serious." That's all I ever learned about that situation. However, the more we talked about her great escapade, the more Bunkie laughed about it; she felt so accomplished. I failed to grasp any of the humor.

Only one other time in my adult life did Bunkie manage to "pull my leg" with such expertise. The first year I worked out of state, the distance from Atlanta created a slight problem. I was unable to comfortably drive home for Thanksgiving and Christmas because of the quick turnaround between the two trips. My plan, therefore, was to skip Thanksgiving because Christmas was the longer of the two holiday breaks. Flying was not a consideration because I had never flown and had no desire to do so. That Thanksgiving was not about to be my first time.

Except for the first two years of my life, Mama, Bunkie, and I had never been apart on either holiday. Propelled by parental instincts to act on my behalf, Bunkie had another plan which she offered in the form of a solemn promise. She would fly to Michigan and join me for Thanksgiving. *Oh, really? Wow!*

Bunkie had never flown anywhere either, at least not by plane; she was a speed demon driving a car, and she never got a ticket. But because she was my mother and it was my first time away from them at a major holiday time, I trusted her. I trusted her promise until her late and last-minute call the night before Thanksgiving. Something had come up demanding her immediate attention early that Friday morning, and she would talk to me about it later. I knew exactly what had come up because I knew my mother. *Nothing!*

Despite our being apart, I had an enjoyable Thanksgiving; and, due to a constant snowfall, I flew home for Christmas. Bunkie continued her promises to fly somewhere with me. *Never did.*

From that experience, I concluded that somewhere in the mix of all the good that Bunkie was and did, a streak of deception was ever constant, most of which seemed reserved for my benefit. Many years later, I determined that deception was Bunkie's way of making less desirable and painful situations easier to bear, or so she thought. She had an enduring stash of "deceptive bandages." Sometimes these bandages backfired or made things worse, but I never let Bunkie know the difference. Mama, her aiding and abetting partner, snitched on Bunkie more than she ever knew. Nevertheless, in tracing these bandages to my childhood, sparing my feelings is the longest memory I have about my mother. The impression is a lasting one because sparing anybody of life's discomforts was the essence of Bunkie's character.

The first time that I remember Bunkie sparing me from discomfort, I was three-and-one-half years old. She sat me on the lap of a man whose face seemed behind a mask. He was Santa Claus, a monstrous looking creature who turned me into a scream machine. Realizing immediately that I was frightened, Bunkie spared my lungs and took me quickly in her arms. The impact of that memory did not last long enough to establish a "Santaphobia." A couple of years later, a teacher dressed all up in a big red suit lost his Santa Claus beard. Another child, in fright, snatched it from his face. I also found out that the real Santa Claus is not a frightening person; I saw her putting the gifts under our Christmas tree.

The memory with the longest impact is about an episode that happened when I was five. The situation resulted in my first exposure to the deceptive bandage, which did not work. Bunkie was teaching out of town, but near enough to come home many weekends. When time came for her to return to work, Mama and I usually went with her to the bus station to see her off.

On one occasion, Bunkie led me to believe that she was taking me with her. As we walked toward the bus for her to take her place in the line of passengers, Bunkie gave me a small package to hold, which slipped through my hands. The bag contained a small bottle of Lysol; and, naturally, it splattered. The little bit of Lysol that spilled onto my shoes was a blessing in disguise for Bunkie, but a disaster for me.

As the people began boarding the bus, I inched along eagerly with Bunkie to the first step up, only to be told that I could not go. Instead, I needed to go home with Mama to clean the Lysol off my shoes. The closer Bunkie got to the inside of the bus, the more I cried; I got louder when the bus pulled off.

Several years later, in talking about that episode, Bunkie confessed that my going with her on that day was never a part of the plan. She further explained that she only said I could go because when I asked, she knew I would cry if she said no. When the topic came up as we talked about my Thanksgiving in Michigan, another disappointment, I never relied solely on my mother's promises again. But I did end up making a deceptive bandage of my own.

Between going to school and job-related activities, I did a lot of solo driving. Most distances were about 600 miles one-way from Atlanta. To spare Mama and Bunkie the frustration of watching the clock for my arrival, to or from my destination, I gave them misinformation. My best revenge was returning home. I had them thinking I would get home anytime between two hours and two days later. I sneaked up behind them in church one Sunday morning. My prize play was returning late one night. They were both asleep. I quietly dressed for bed and greeted them the next morning.

Afterthought

In words that I heard only from Bunkie, "It's a bad wind that never changes." Bunkie was the wind in my life that propelled me to everything good in life. She never changed. But, then, love never does. Think about it. . . .

Any memory of love is a lasting impression!

Part Two

Climbing from the Mountaintop

One Flag, Two Flags, Three Flags, Four . . .

Adult friends who have not seen each other in twenty or more years tend to greet each other with a mutually exchanged compliment: "You haven't changed a bit!" Entirely disregarded is all proof of a weight gain or loss of five to fifty pounds, hairpieces or partial to total baldness, dentures or gum space once occupied by two or more teeth, aromas of cologne mixed with Ben Gay, and an age increase, probably ignored since their thirty-ninth birthday. Nevertheless, there is a great sense of pride and joy in resembling enough of what used to be, thereby allowing them to be recognized at all. Some friends do not have the luxury of being recognized after a long time of absence because of massive physical change.

Whether for better or worse, the human aging process is nurtured by change almost daily from the time we are born. Change is the reason we shed our baby teeth and replace our second set with dentures. Pending our life span, some kind of visible change also takes place in our mental health and behavior.

Some change in the aging process is expected and, therefore, more easily accepted. But when the down slope of life imposes an unexpected challenge as part of our personal agenda from which there is no escape, the emotional reality of acceptance takes on a field of related inexperience. Such is the dramatic entrance and impact of Alzheimer's disease, the type of dementia encountered by my mother. Somehow, something suddenly goes terribly wrong that gravely reduces the capacity of mental functions. Due to a number of factors, the mind, as the control center of behavior, progressively transfers from a level of normality to one of abnormality. Accordingly, some victims and their family members unknowingly engage in periods of anger, denial, frustration, or pretense prior to reaching a state of genuine acceptance.

No Color, No Flag

Bunkie was clever in rousing my curiosity with lead-in statements that she had faked purposely to get information from me. If I were unaware of a particular situation, but wanted her to tell me more, Bunkie would bring the conversation to an abrupt halt. Ending the conversation did not bother me half as much as the inferring air of her closing statement: "Well, I won't say any more about that. We'll just wait." Bunkie may well have been trying to pick my brain, but it usually appeared that she knew the "juicy" details and had no intention of sharing them. An inquiring mind does not handle such rejection well. Piquing my curiosity was also one of her ways of setting me up for one of her pranks.

Other times, if I were absorbed in a meaningful task and failed to remember something because of my preoccupation at the time or the matter not being important to me, the results were the same. Rather than giving me hints or being more detailed, Bunkie left me puzzling my brain, having interrupted my great moments of concentration.

There were also just as many times when Bunkie began statements without completing them. After a long pause, I would utter impatiently, *"and?"* After more hesitation, she would finally respond, indicating we would talk about it at a later time. Bunkie was a regular "later" person.

That particular tendency was more frequent in my adult life, and pre-existed her death by more than twenty years. Could it have been the prelude to Alzheimer's? If so, any waving flag was recognized as reflecting nothing more than her true character.

The defining moment of Bunkie's onset of dementia was quite easy to recognize about five years after its beginning. Before that fifth year, any flags of warning simply had no visible colors; least of all were they red.

My failure to fully detect or even suspect any symptom of Alzheimer's in Bunkie's behavior was much like my first eye examination in 1968. Printed words literally jumped around whenever I attempted to read. The exam required that I view an enlarged "E" through a screening device. At that point, the optometrist instructed me to inform him as soon as the E began separating into two Es. By the time I saw the double E form, one E was one side of the room and the other E was far away, on the other side of the room. The optometrist quickly emphasized that there was no human way my vision could be so poor. We later determined that my vision was being impaired or compromised by medication that I had taken for a few days about a week before the exam.

In like manner, the problem with detecting Bunkie's onset of Alzheimer's rested in the frequency of her odd behavior and my rationalizing each episode. More specifically, Bunkie's normal behavior was much more constant compared to her rare spurts of "peculiar" behavior, which, therefore, compromised detecting any measure of dementia. By virtue of her nature, the onset of her abnormal tendencies made it more appropriate to rationalize her behavior than anything else. And that's the way I went; after all, I grew up rationalizing Bunkie's behavior.

As early as 1992, while reminiscing old family times, I questioned Bunkie about Uncle Jake's arm. Uncle Jake was her then-deceased stepbrother who lost an arm early in his life, and I was interested in what caused that misfortune. Bunkie's response caused me concern initially. She indicated no awareness of Uncle Jake being one-armed. I pursued the matter briefly, realizing that she knew differently. Uncle Jake and his one-armed self had stayed with us in recent years, though for a few days. There were also other times when we had been together at family gatherings. But Bunkie never changed her response. She did question me, however; "Who told you Jake had just one arm?"

Being accustomed to Bunkie's ways of concealing information, I decided the matter of how Uncle Jake lost his arm may have involved details that Bunkie felt were better left unsaid. The possibility of any truth in that thought made it easy for me to further believe that her denial was a way of telling me to drop the subject. Her manner of dismissing my concern was in keeping with her style; it was normal behavior. Shutting down was her reaction when I asked her to talk to me about my father. Nothing had happened to him. I was curious because I never knew him or anything about him. So when everything is normal, there's no need for flag hunting. Hunting is reserved for the less complicated elements of life, such as Easter eggs, and some of them are hard enough to find.

Evidence of a real flag surfaced three years later. The revealing episode, however, was somewhat connected to a previous event.

Upon returning from a meeting one day in the summer of 1994, Bunkie discovered our home had been invaded. She was alone at the time, and I was thirty miles away, participating in a bowling tournament. My bedroom was the only room disturbed; a few small items were taken, one of which had sentimental value and was probably thought to contain money because it was locked.

Two things were rather strange about that situation, one being Bunkie's calm demeanor. The fact that we had never experienced a break-in made her calmness odd because her tremors, effected by Parkinson's, should have been, at least, visible. The magnitude of her shaking always intensified under extraordinary circumstances; sometimes ordinary fit the bill. But her head and arms never trembled, even as she talked with the police. Neither was there any quivering in her voice, which was also an effect of her Parkinson's.

Secondly, the point of entry was another bedroom which was untouched in the "little robbery," except for the broken window. The intruder even took time to prop the screen against the window, adjust the curtains and drapes, and reposition a little table that had to have been in the way.

In view of my mom's calmness throughout the aftermath, and just knowing her tactics in handling urgencies, our home invasion became more puzzling than disturbing, and one particular piece never fit; in no way did Bunkie's calm fit the occasion of a robbery. Furthermore, as much as she could talk about "big happenings," she never spoke of that incident again with me or, to my knowledge, anybody else either. My conclusion was, therefore, plain and simple.

Beginning with her retirement, Bunkie was known for not keeping up with her house key. Sometimes, when the key was in her purse she was unable to find it there. Basically, she seldom needed her key anyway. Usually, when she went somewhere, especially at that time in her life, the two of us were together; I was the first in the house because Bunkie took her time getting out of the car, and not for physical reasons. Sometimes a notable Atlanta Brave was at bat on the radio.

Bunkie was also known for prying a slightly loose glass panel in our kitchen door to get in the house because she had either forgotten, or couldn't find, her key.

I concluded, therefore, that she forgot her key on the day of the incident and hailed a small-bodied person to break into our home. She was probably too unsteady to maneuver the loose glass panel in our kitchen door because of her tremors but cautious enough to not make whomever aware of that particular slat. Instead, she allowed the person to break a roll-out glass panel from one of our windows. The person had to be thin to crawl through the window. Once inside, that person took the most suitable items found in a quick search.

Two of our immediate neighbors had tools taken from their carports a few weeks within the time of our incident. Those thefts were also first-time incidents.

Several weeks later, a male teenager, arrested in an unrelated incident, confessed to our three neighborhood thefts. His identity was withheld because his confession was unsolicited and given in the absence of an attorney. My neighbors and I were probably correct in speculating his identity, and I was probably correct in speculating that he managed to get into our home with Bunkie's help.

Oddly enough, about three years later, Bunkie suddenly began telling a few friends and church members that someone had broken into our home. By the time I knew of her continued reports, Bunkie was indicating that our home had "just" been broken into seven times. Each time she spoke of the incident, the seven break-ins had always occurred within the same week of her report. She talked about our "recent" break-ins for more than a year, but not constantly, just every now and then, mostly every then.

Reality Happens, Flag or No Flag

For reasons of her own, Bunkie never mentioned the break-ins in my presence. In the latter months of her "misinforming" the public, I spent time trying to catch her in the act. When opportunity came for me to hear (and maybe correct) her, Bunkie was so adamant in giving details and responding to me that I stood motionless, in shock! Being agitated, especially in public, was rare for Bunkie, and I had never liked seeing her in that state of mind. But once I actually heard her relating tales of our home invasion, I took immediate action! The full and only extent of my one-step action was hoping that Bunkie would bring an end to her journalistic practice of imagination before I believed her myself. She was so convincing. Even so, her behavior did result in an unforeseen flag crashing my unbelief, and I accepted its presence, but only one flag was in my viewing range.

The less Bunkie talked of the nonhappening break-ins, the more the flag disintegrated into thin air. The ultimate reality of my hope was achieved when Bunkie finally stopped talking about the break-ins. Hence, no more flag; not a red flag anyway. I erased the burning red hue each of the four times I succeeded in getting her to remember the time we really had a break-in; if we really did.

Only two other major episodes of Bunkie's behavior occurred that positively substantiated that her mental capacity was, indeed, failing. The first of the two had the greatest impact on my emotions. The day was Sunday, July 26, 1998.

I had coordinated an appreciation program for our pastor, Rev. Dr. Robert Green. The program participants had done an outstanding job in their performances. Amid the many compliments expressed, Bunkie never said anything to me. As we drove home from the program, I asked what she thought about it. She only responded, "It was all right."

That response was so shallow and out of character for her that only one explanation was possible. She may not have been aware of what was going on. The dual purpose of the program as a formal appreciation and farewell presented not one, but two topics of discussion for Bunkie. She spoke of neither during our ride home. As far as I know, Bunkie never discussed the program with anyone, but she did talk a lot about Rev. Green's new pastoral appointment in unrelated conversations.

On that Sunday, July 26, 1998, I didn't need "the flag of reality" to make me a believer. For the first time in my life, I knew that the mental presence of my ever faithful and abiding cheerleader was missing. Bunkie's dementia was a reality; it just wasn't constant. Nevertheless, that day was the beginning of our climb up the down side of dementia.

A year later, I was in the second year of my confirmation to the Steward Board at my church, and was the new chairman. Bunkie was at least a twenty-year veteran member of the same board, and quite vocal in an indirect way.

For several years, Bunkie tended to mumble disapproval so as not to be heard by the entire body. As her Alzheimer's progressed, she became louder with such mumblings. In our November meeting, as I gently stroked Bunkie's shoulder to quiet her mumblings, she blasted me **real** good; *"You shut up!"*

Fortunately, the members were aware of her mental decline, and were sympathetic. That particular instance of her violent outburst was the first and last done publicly. It would be the only one that she willingly talked about with the presence of mind to apologize.

One Step at a Time, One Day at a Time

As children, a few of my friends and I got our kicks from abusing the purpose for which escalators are used. There was no excitement or fun greater than walking the steps in the opposite direction. Half the gain we made in each step forward was lost in two steps backward. Our thrilling effort was spent prolonging the joy of that challenge by walking as slowly as we could, for reaching another floor was neither our intention nor purpose.

In some respects, dementia, in the form of Alzheimer's disease, is the antithesis of our dangerous play on escalators; it is neither excitement nor fun. Throughout its natural course, Alzheimer's allows no choice of final destination. As my caregiving experience, Alzheimer's was an unfortunate peak of our mountain range. Bunkie and I managed the downward journey, however, by climbing one step at a time, one day at a time. Since bypassing that peak to reach our original mountain top was not even a remote possibility, the challenge of climbing from the mountain top was similar to that of my childhood escalator rides. Bunkie and I took our steps together in the opposite direction for as long as we could.

The total experience of climbing up the down side of dementia with my mom never involved taking risks. But the climb, itself, was a joint venture that remains unforgettable from several perspectives.

Blazing New Turf

A sore throat, antibiotic intakes, and a few days of in-termittent rest equal the onset, duration, and end of a summer or winter cold. Unfortunately, most types of de-mentia are not so neatly packaged or timed. Warnings as-sociated with Alzheimer's do not become distinct in such a brief period of time; neither do they occur at a particular time or in a specific way. For some warnings, a human's age range may or may not be significant as a determining factor. The behavior of children makes a strong case in this regard.

Prior to a more sophisticated and compassionate re-gard for mental disorders, a mind was easy to lose at any age. Children, in my growing up years, lost their minds on a daily basis. At least some of our parents thought so and expressed that thought at home and in public. In re-sponse to our sudden desires, spurts of misbehavior, and binges of pouting, they often wondered whether we had lost our minds.

Detecting the onset of dementia in Bunkie's behavior was not as easy as may be expected. Only in retrospect can a time table of occurrence be assessed, which extends her onset of dementia over a five-year span (1993–1998). Bunkie's symptomatic behavior during those years was brief and sporadic without much change in her topical emphases. Her longest preoccupations held her focus on our unreal home invasions and securing a substantial home equity loan that we did not need. In the absence of any direct or indirect medical confirmation, I only knew that, from time to time, Bunkie's behavior was inconsis-tently strange and out of character.

The reason Bunkie was never diagnosed with demen-tia was almost simple. Until her case of Alzheimer's was noticeably advanced, she was always on her best mental behavior in the presence of her doctor(s). Bunkie would have probably discounted any previous diagnosis about her mental health anyway. Her regular doctors knew her so well that they may have even speculated that possibility.

Bunkie had an outstanding medical history of not following through on recommendations, referrals, and taking prescribed medicine. She was also deliberate in withholding pertinent information about her health from me and her doctors. Only by incident, during one of her doctor's appointments in 1996, did I know my mom had been diagnosed with Parkinson's in the early 1960s and had rejected treatment. I just concluded all along that she had some kind of nervous condition because of her tremors, which progressed slowly over thirty years.

Bunkie's personal health was just that, *personal!* She always indicated that she had her time set for dealing with whatever ailment she had, and she did—most times, *never!* I learned many years before Bunkie's declining health to remain relatively passive about her health; she could be quite aggressive and stubborn in that regard. I never had need to override her personal health decisions until the last year she lived.

In March of 2000, after two years of her flirting with a bladder infection, I requested hospital personnel to give her an antibiotic injection because she never took her medicine long enough to clear the infection. At the time of my request, Bunkie had pretended to take two pills; ten minutes later, the pills were still in her mouth. She probably would have ultimately spit them out once our heads were turned. During and after the scuffle of giving her the injection, Bunkie was "royally" displeased with the hospital staff and me, and was quite demonstrative in showing

74

her displeasure. But the better she felt after the shot, the happier she was in discussing and joking about the episode.

At some point near the end of her five-year onset of dementia, I realized that part of accepting her declining mental state required a "newness" on my part. As a starter, I became more vigilant in expecting the "unexpected." Sooner than I realized, the frustration generated by her peak moments of erratic behavior was minimized significantly. That step was my first down the mountain with Bunkie; our morale, though sometimes up and sometimes down, prevailed as a positive factor to the end of our climb.

Alzheimer's disease is a constant unfolding drama of dementia that commands first-time adaptations throughout its progressive course. Regardless of how many or few adjustments are needed, each one creates a new experience for all immediate persons affected. At least, that was my discovery. The greater the frequency and intensity of Bunkie's abnormal behavior, the more the two of us were about the business of blazing new turf together. In the process, Bunkie became a born-again strategist; to meet the challenge of her strategies, so did I.

The Back Streets of Camouflage and Sham

Chances of being stuck in major traffic jams anywhere in metropolitan Atlanta are as common as those of seeing referees at professional football games. The inch-by-inch crawl in stalling traffic was less frustrating with Bunkie in the car because I knew that we would soon escape the jam. Bunkie knew just about every back street there was to know in Atlanta. But when college students from all over the nation converged in Atlanta, getting to the back streets took a number of years. At least, the hassle made it seem that way.

Traffic during the one million people "freaknik" celebrations in Atlanta was a living nightmare that creatures of sanity tried to avoid. Interstate exit ramps were officially barricaded as far as ten miles in every direction to and from the downtown areas. Police were stationed every two or three ramps. As an add-on feature, the travel rate in the hype of freaknik traffic was half a mile per two hours, and that's not an exaggeration.

One year, Bunkie and I were delayed three or more hours in freaknik traffic while en route to a local hospital. Our next-door neighbor had been transported to that hospital from a wreck a few hours earlier, and we wanted to check on her. We finally got within a block of the hospital, only to be rerouted to the interstate.

The round-trip time between our home and the hospital, normally half an hour, was becoming longer and longer by hours. In the next hour that it took for us to reach the first policed ramp after being rerouted, Bunkie got the policeman's attention and explained our dilemma. Five minutes or less, we were free of the interstate. Our exit led us into unfamiliar territory. Thanks to Bunkie's keen sense of direction, we steered our way from those back streets to downtown Atlanta.

Since Bunkie and I were the only two people traveling downtown Atlanta that night, the experience was weird; the whole downtown area was just like a ghost town. But compared to being stuck on the interstate, the downtown and back streets of Atlanta on that night were the next best thing to crispy brown fried chicken. The funeral home was second best; Bunkie and I stopped at one on the way home because I needed to use the rest room.

Back streets or alternate routes are also crucial to navigating other kinds of life situations. Bunkie traveled an alternate route in life longer than thirty years because of Parkinson's disease. By 1980, she was a pro at navigating the back street of "Camouflage Boulevard." Her first public strategy was creating a need to leave during our communion service because of her difficulty in handling the bread and "wine." Counteracting her strategy, I began sitting with Bunkie during communion and assisted as she was communed at her seat. Eventually, she felt comfortable with the newness of her situation and never left the service again, even when we were not sitting together.

While making adjustments in her public life, Bunkie had already begun using a plastic jar-shaped container at home for drinking beverages. She bragged on her new "personal glass" because it held a couple more ounces. The truth was that the canister was easier to hold. As her muscular deterioration progressed, Bunkie eventually used drinking straws as a result of my trickery or fibbing. She also resorted to eating out of tin pans instead of porcelain plates.

The ability to write was also among the first physical abilities that Bunkie lost completely to Parkinson's; her penmanship had always been so beautiful. When she was no longer able to read her writing, Bunkie became more skilled in remembering telephone numbers and other data that she would have normally jotted down for future reference.

Beginning in 1993, the memory system that Bunkie had so expertly groomed and relied upon to compensate for her writing handicap was gradually faded by Alzheimer's. Before being completely bumped from the highway of mental retention, Bunkie somehow recognized the need to make another detour in her life. From that point on, Bunkie gave all incoming disabilities her best shot. The trickery so true to her character was still in tow as she relocated a little further up on Camouflage Boulevard to the corner of "Sham Avenue." From that intersection, Bunkie navigated the main course of life for almost six years. She rearmed herself with modified tactics and started firing her final round of shots about October of 1998.

For a great number of years prior to 1998, Bunkie had a standard way of greeting people whom she had not seen or heard from in awhile. In response to those concerned about how she had been getting along, her immediate statement was, "Who wants to know?" with emphasis on "who." That question became another classic signature of her character. Every now and then she asked very boldly, with her charming smile, "And who are you, and where did you come from?" The intent was to let others know that they had been out of touch too long, if only for a week, and that she was glad to see or hear from them.

Many times since Bunkie died, some of our friends have called out to me, *Who wants to know!* as if that were my real name; each time, I loved every minute of the downpour of memories.

In 1998, however, Bunkie's custom of asking "Who wants to know?" began to take on new meaning. She **really** wanted to know, because her ability to identify people by name was failing. As usual, talking to whomever was definitely not a problem for her at the time. She just wanted to know to whom she was talking without it being known that she really didn't know.

Family and church matters had always been her main topics of conversation for hours at a time. Since all of our friends were members of a church and most had children, Bunkie shammed with her lead-in question; "How are those children?" She kept the church in reserve until conversations about the children had run their course. Later on, when we were alone, she asked me the names of those with whom she had talked. That strategy worked until her final days. Listening to her conversations was amusing because of the way in which she shammed her mental presence to others. She worked her strategy flawlessly and with such a convincing surface.

An earlier strategy that Bunkie devised for giving me telephone messages did not work for her nearly as long, but was equally amusing. She began the message with a series of questions. In turn, each answer I gave was actually part of the message. Anywhere between five to ten questions later, I had the entire message. The great task of Bunkie naming the caller was as clever as cleverness gets. I actually found myself doing a roll call of my friends for her. But first, I needed the caller's most frequently known environmental setting: educational, religious, commercial, or residential. For example, the educational setting meant calling out the names of my closest colleagues. Commercial was the easiest for Bunkie to handle because usually the contact was from my car dealership. Bunkie also assisted the process in her attempts to identify the caller by complexion, weight, and height, clothes, hair, or voice. Once she heard the person's name, both of us, as well as the caller, had hit a million dollar jackpot. "That's the one!" she would exclaim.

When that strategy lost its power and purpose a year or two later, it didn't matter whose name I called; the right one never popped up. Eventually, I alerted friends, colleagues, and others to the need for them to talk directly with me rather than leave a message. One time much later, when a friend called me about an urgent matter, Bunkie not only forgot the caller's name and the message, she forgot that I was in my bedroom. By that time, I had matured way beyond the point of previous frustration. Bunkie and I had a good time laughing about the incident.

Dynamics of the Heart and Mind

The total experience of my involvement in Bunkie's bout with dementia can be broken into three stages, the first and longest of which was the onset. The intermediate stage was next and, perhaps, the most brief. The time span of that stage may have been hastened by Bunkie's age and the increasingly rapid effects of Parkinson's as well as Alzheimer's. The advanced stage was the ultimate or final stage. Primary factors of separation for each stage included a higher level of identifiable differences in the nature, frequency, and duration of Bunkie's periods of demented behavior.

From a reactionary point of view, I further suggest that the onset of dementia is a fostering and harboring stage. It's the best spot where family, friends, and even the victim can persist unguardedly with anger, denial, defiance, naivety, doubt, and hope.

The intermediate stage is set in motion by the first day of unpretentious reckoning with an episode of dementia, particularly on the part of a spouse, parent, or the adult child. The first day is the point of accepting reality unconditionally, and also begins the period for making multi-purpose adjustments for the proverbial long road ahead. Finding a comfort zone for nurturing physical and emotional survival must be top priority because the victim's most conscious efforts are directed toward maintaining independence and a sense of control. Unfortunately, the victim no longer has a consistent mental capacity to accommodate total freedom or self-control. Consequently, frustration escalates with each episode of dementia or it either comes and goes until it finally stays gone.

The advanced stage merely inherits the highest degree of all the victim's disordered behaviors. Once on the stage of finality, the mind's grip on sanity at this point in dementia is either totally or almost totally lost.

Rebellion between the victim and others is more prominent in the onset and intermediate stages. A main feature of the transition between the intermediate and advanced stages is reversal of roles between victimized parents and their adult children. When dementia reaches the advanced stage, only in the victim are dynamics of the heart and mind bound to opposition in a tug of war. Oftentimes the mind, on the spur of the moment, abandons the heart.

The harsh reality of knowing that dementia is in full force makes it all the more evident that the victim's mind is relentless in irrational and crude pursuits, whether those pursuits are in behavior or thought. The heart doesn't stand a chance in the heap of mental distortions, and only awaits return of a calm demeanor. Until that calm returns, the heart is no match for the mind. Neither is the heart responsible for abnormal activity ordered or conducted by the mind. For that reason, any direct or indirect display of insulting or offensive behavior by the victim should not be interpreted by family members or others as a personal attack.

On a brighter side, however, the advanced stage is also the point where love, patience, and understanding prevail as the biggest payoff, pending the relationship and interaction between the victim and all others. Bunkie and I became second-time billionaires!

Reckoning day can be restrained in the background of dementia for just so long. Though my mom and I climbed onto the intermediate stage in 1998, her show of dementia was still a bit too puny for me to make or accept a full declaration in that respect. After all, she was still into "shamming" her way through life. By my standards, Bunkie needed to be more daily, more hourly, or more *anything* than she was. Christmas Eve of 1998 made me glad that she wasn't! Without any doubt, in that day, my true day of reckoning fully with the reality of Bunkie's dementia had arrived and was probably the twentieth to arrive by that time.

Bunkie had a sudden and unexplained urgency to see one of her doctors, whose office was located thirty or more miles from our home. In addition to being Christmas Eve, that day was the second of an accumulated snowfall.

One must first understand that being merely alerted to the possibility of a single snowflake falling in Atlanta, big or small, is historically an almost rare event that clears all grocery store shelves of bread and milk. Whenever a predicted snowflake actually falls, any mode of transportation is a life-taking risk. A snowfall of two or more flakes is too much for all of metropolitan Atlanta and far more damaging; we become snowbound!

The only available medical attention for local citizens and visitors on that Christmas Eve, even had it been just another day, could only be received at the emergency room of a local hospital. Such a fully operating facility was less than ten minutes from our kitchen door, nine minutes and forty-eight seconds from our driveway, nine-and-one-half minutes from the first main street nearest to our home, and excluded three minutes for parking and walking into the hospital. The nearest hospital to our home was, therefore, no more than seven minutes away. Moreover, the route to that hospital was red-light free. By comparison, Bunkie's urgent preference required longer than two hours for the round-trip distance because of the snow and ice.

Unable to reason with Bunkie about the holiday and its snowfall, we set out on our journey to her doctor's office at a snail's pace. She even disregarded the recorded message informing callers that the office was closed. I gave in because she became irritable and threatened to call a cab and anybody else to take her to that doctor.

About twenty miles into the trip, Bunkie read the interstate signs which indicated exit lanes to Augusta, Georgia, and Greenville, South Carolina. She wanted to know immediately where we were going. I answered her without expressing my own level of irritation. We had traveled that same route to that same doctor several times. Shortly after my response, Bunkie commented, in the manner of a first-time traveler, that had she known the trip was that far, she would not have come.

In my silent fury, I was even more determined to complete the journey, if for no other reason than for Bunkie to see the snow-covered parking lot of her doctor's closed office. We had about twenty more minutes to go at the time. When we arrived at the complex that housed the doctor's office, the parking lot was full of snow and ice patches. No other car was in sight.

After parallel parking close to the doctor's ground-level office door, I even proceeded to ring the doorbell, which completed my mission of proving a point as Bunkie watched. I am sure that my point was proven in vain. Nevertheless, we drove home in silence, except for the Christmas carols on the radio.

Later on that evening as Bunkie talked on the telephone about our trip, she said, almost gloating, that she forgot it was Christmas Eve. I knew instantly that my days of doubt, naivety, and denial were over. My day of reckoning with reality had come. But I still was not ready to commit to acceptance; it was so much easier to be frustrated. So I proceeded to be frustrated with my mother on three more occasions. Incidentally, the next time Bunkie went to the doctor, she chose one of her doctors who was about ten minutes away. Her next visit was in late February the next year. The day was snowless.

Patching New Fabric with Old Thread

Human experience is perhaps the best teacher of human behavior. In one way or another, we are able to connect the massive range of personality traits that simultaneously bind and separate our sameness as individuals to all situational behavior. Just as no two people within the scope of normal behavior are exactly the same, dementia in one person's behavior is unique to that person's character and, therefore, not the same in another victim's behavior. Therein accounted for is the human factor of dementia. But the fact that every human being is the same in some kind of way completes the paradox of dementia being inherently the same in each case of its victim's behavior; each victim has a disordered state of mind.

The main truth of that premise is all people (the normal and abnormal) are first human, but in that human sameness, each person is uniquely different. Accordingly, the slightest of differences in cases of a normal or abnormal state of mind adds quality to the age-old saying, "Different strokes for different folks."

Among the most common of symptoms associated with Alzheimer's, those most dominant in Bunkie's behavior were mostly erratic extensions of her previous normal state of mind; they were unique to her former character. The aforementioned situation of her determination to get to her faraway doctor on a snow-patched holiday reflected her former character of mental strength and self determination.

Bunkie's show of determination was closer to being a century strong. One of her most urgent acts of assertiveness was her first attempt ever to secure a driver's license in 1968. After failing her first state driver's exam, she even approached me to get her a license in Michigan. Evidently, I was far from being her last hope. Though I have no idea how Bunkie ever got a driver's license in her then current stage of Parkinson's, it was legally renewed every four years thereafter.

Surprisingly enough, Bunkie kept up with her expiration date religiously. Her last renewal was in 1997. By that year, Bunkie had stopped driving on her own. As I indicated to the issuing officials that her license would only be used for identification, Bunkie confirmed happily and added that she had not driven in two months. *Wrong by reason of dementia!* Occasionally, I reminded Bunkie that she had not driven since September of 1996, following what could have easily been a fatal automobile accident. Either she blacked out at the wheel or the ignition cut off, resulting in her coasting across a busy street and onto a lawn full of big trees because she was physically and mentally unable to handle the car.

A big problem of dementia for an independent and assertive person, such as my mother was, is giving up control unless the need is projected with crystal clarity. Bunkie realized the need to stop driving in 1996 and made an appropriate and wise decision. Two years later, on Christmas Eve, her behavioral difference was the lack of mental ability to exercise appropriate judgment at a primary level. Whereas our driveway was a dangerous place to be because of snow and ice accumulation, Bunkie did not consider the imposing threat of danger from driving so far a distance to her doctor during inclement weather conditions. Most of all, she failed to remember that private physicians and their staff close up shop for major holidays, especially Christmas Eve.

As a disclosure of personal strength, Bunkie's type of remissive behavior in another person's case of dementia might have had more or less intensity with different consequences. By the same token, workable solutions in response to one person's case of dementia may prove totally inappropriate or unsuccessful in responding to another person's case. One intervening factor is the victim's former presence of character. In a sense, the victim doesn't fall too far from his or her tree, of personality, that is.

Three Spools of Adjustment

Following her Christmas Eve episode in 1998, Bunkie was mostly episode-free, and remained mentally aware until early February of the next year. Thereafter, her gradual show of confusion and forgetfulness became more standard and stretched into a sixteen-month series of activity. Meanwhile, for the first time since her onset of dementia, Bunkie's episodes were slightly predictable. When they didn't happen, the greatest sensation was releasing my breath in relief.

About March of that year, I was finally on my way to graduating "some kind of laude" from frustration to full acceptance of Bunkie's mental limitations. But we had three more advanced courses to take, however fictitious. The first was "Principles of Upgrading the Togetherness Factor."

Most of Bunkie's six credit card bills were due by the

sixth of each month. Due to her Parkinson's, I had helped by writing her checks since the eighties. As Bunkie's mental health began changing more rapidly in 1999, so did the preparations for paying her bills:

1. Bunkie wanted to see each check as soon as it was written. *No problem.*

2. After all six checks were written, Bunkie wanted to see all six checks. *No problem.*

3. After putting each check with the remittance slip in the envelope, Bunkie wanted to see each check and remittance slip. *Almost a problem.*

4. After sealing and stamping the six envelopes containing one check and remittance slip each, Bunkie wanted to see each check and remittance slip again. *Whoa! A great big, huge and monumental problem!*

But I was cool. I managed to be frustrated with patience throughout Bunkie's two-hour inspection period. In addition to that bit of maturity in me, I also detected by the time I adjusted to one level or phase of Bunkie's dementia that the time had come for yet another adjustment, and the needs for readjusting were becoming more frequent and rapid. I was almost a seamstress in the process; making sudden adjustments was the same as changing spools of thread.

After two months of Bunkie's routine inspection of checks and remittance slips, I decided we needed to use a stronger thread of togetherness. I invited Bunkie to keep up with the envelopes, stamps, and remittance slips; tell me the amount to write for each check and to whom the check should be made payable; and stack each check with its remittance slip and envelope. After all checks were written, I sat next to Bunkie as we looked at the checks and remittance slips together before sealing them in the envelopes. Next, I helped her place the envelopes in her pocketbook, and off we went to the post office. That routine inspection took half the time. It also made Bunkie feel needed and special.

We followed that routine until March of 2000. A few months before that time, Bunkie felt well enough to pay her bills in person. That meant going to three banks on the same day to join the host of other Atlantans also paying their bills the first of the month. *No problem!* Bunkie was in total control and not in need of my assistance. I had already written her checks; therefore, my work was done.

Prior to 1997, Bunkie usually paid her bills in person. So most bank personnel knew Bunkie, and they knew her mannerisms. For the two years leading up to 1997, Bunkie had stopped standing in the teller's line. She went directly from the main entrance to "her" desk or office where her "regular" personnel who waited on her were already busy assisting other customers with loans, new accounts, and other business matters. Bunkie unintentionally ignored the fact that she had bypassed at least three or more people sitting in a designated area each time, waiting to be called on in the order of their arrival. But no harm was ever done.

The customers and bank personnel were very, very kind and extremely patient. After all, Bunkie had greeted everybody with a radiant smile as she entered. She bid those still around and any newcomer good-bye in the same manner; but added, "You all take care now and have a good good day!" On her healthier days, she would turn around and wave again to everybody from the door.

A few weeks after Bunkie died, I visited with some of the bank and hospital personnel who had regularly waited on her to thank them for the respect and kindness they always showed my mother. In each instance, upon learning about Bunkie's death, the employees were overcome with grief. Bunkie had a growing impact on people with whom she dealt. She loved them and it showed; they loved her back.

Change continued to develop in Bunkie's mental and physical health throughout the remainder of 1999, leaving nothing to be ignored. Alzheimer's was a bit more rampant in attacking her mind, while Parkinson's began a swifter stampede on her muscular frame. Despite a more significant decline in her health, Bunkie retained her ability to sham a good while longer; but even her best shamming was not up to *her* usual par. Except for going to the bathroom and bedding down for the night, Bunkie began confining herself to our den for well-pretended reasons. No doubt, some of the pretense behind that confinement was Bunkie's way of reserving her physical strength without talking about it. She also had greater access to me and the bigger of two television screens.

On an occasion closer to mid-year of 1999, Bunkie vaguely expressed fear of being alone at home. A couple of hours before commenting on her fear, there had been a severe thunderstorm that I waited out at the bowling alley. Though the storm was a long and frightening experience and maybe an isolated case of jitters for Bunkie, I took her fear seriously. There was slight indication that she may have become disoriented during the storm. For that reason, I never left her alone at home again if rain were in the forecast. I also decided against beginning the 1999–2000 bowling season with my Monday morning league. Dropping all my bowling activities would have definitely increased our time together.

Upon learning about my decision, Bunkie questioned my reason for giving up bowling. She knew how much I enjoyed my league. The more I explained the three-hour block for league was more time than I wanted for her to be alone, the more she "ordered" me to continue my league participation. Bunkie added to her case with two reminders: league was usually over by noon and, since she was a late sleeper, she would just be getting up for the day about the time of my return home. In response to my suggestion that Helen, our cousin, stay with her on my league mornings, Bunkie assured me that she would be okay. Her exact comment was, "You stay with your league. I'll be all right. If I need you, I know how to call you."

The new bowling season started with a big blast that September, the week after Labor Day. I stayed with my league and called Bunkie twice every Monday morning from the bowling alley. The second call was to let her know that I was on my way home and to find out if she wanted anything from the store. Sometimes, as a joke, Bunkie asked on the second call whether I had already changed my shoes, and laughed. She was remembering the many times I called her from bowling tournaments to say I was on my way home as soon as I put my shoes on, only to call her back within ten minutes to tell her that I was about to bowl another shift, and that I would call again as soon as the shift was over.

The year of 1999 was a different kind of year and a different kind of time for Bunkie and me. I kept my time at the bowling alley to a new bare minimum and never stayed later than my second call. The new spool of adjustment that we started using earlier in April lasted until bowling season was over, almost nine months later. Our stronger thread of togetherness never broke.

Bunkie's "days of sham" came to an end in November 1999. By that time, our den had become her living quarters for doing everything from bathing to sleeping. Both diseases were beginning their final run to the finish line; the advanced stage of each was begun. Parkinson's limited Bunkie's walking capacity to a snail's pace, and her episodes of dementia were more frequent. In addition to those effects, Bunkie's vision was becoming more impaired by cataracts.

Nothing was new about Bunkie's problems with her eyesight; that was also one of her health problems that she had ignored for several years. Bunkie had been diagnosed with cataracts on three occasions, each time by a different optometrist. The first diagnosis was in the early eighties, the second, almost ten years later. Each time, in her natural way, Bunkie ignored referrals to an ophthalmologist with the claim that she only needed some reading glasses. Furthermore, Bunkie never intended for anybody to, as she would say, "mess" with her eyes.

In the fall of 1998, after talking with friends about their cataract surgery and admitting that her vision was blurred, Bunkie finally kept an appointment with an ophthalmologist. She even got her wish and more. Glasses were prescribed, but with further diagnosis of cataracts and a recommendation for surgery. Her exam also showed a trace of glaucoma. Bunkie was only concerned about getting a pair of reading glasses; anything else discussed was less than insignificant.

Thrilled at the prospect of Bunkie having prescribed glasses, I paid the full amount for the glasses instead of the minimum nonrefundable fee required. When we went to pick the glasses up ten days later, Bunkie declared that she couldn't "see a thing." The office staff was nice enough to refund all my money. They understood Bunkie and the nature of my problem. In all probability, Bunkie decided against taking the glasses because her tremors made it extremely difficult for her to handle putting them on and taking them off. Over a ten-year period, she had broken two pairs of Mama's old glasses and three pairs of mine. Hopefully, reading was Bunkie's primary need for glasses.

Bunkie also rejected another aid that should have increased her comfort. After rolling her up and down our hallway a few times on my stereo table, I borrowed a wheelchair for Bunkie, thinking it would be a pleasant surprise. The fact that my presentation of the wheelchair did not work out in the way I planned is an understatement. I was the one surprised by Bunkie's reaction; "You want me to sit in that thing and die?"

After three months of coaxing Bunkie in vain, I returned the wheelchair. The only wheelchair service that Bunkie accepted graciously was at the doctor's office and church.

The challenge of assisting Bunkie with preparing her monthly bills was easy compared to other challenges that mounted during the year of 1999. Without much warning, the simple things to do in life became increasingly difficult for Bunkie. But I was more gamed than ever with confidence! I had emotionally arrived! Nothing could happen or be so drastic in Bunkie's behavior that God, Bunkie, and I could not handle with a few adjustments.

Between Alzheimer's and Parkinson's, Bunkie eventually lost the mental and motor skills needed to operate her two longest luxuries of life, the telephone and television. Operating the television became more of a serious problem as early as 1997 with Bunkie's progressive inability to be steady when using the remote control. The solution to that problem was quick and easy.

The first step was buying the largest remote panel available. The larger an object was, the easier it was for Bunkie to hold or use. We kept two remotes on hand because Bunkie and I often dropped them. The same two we had are still in one piece and operable. The next step, whenever Bunkie was alone at home, was my leaving the television on and already set on the channel Bunkie watched most. The CBS network was usually good for entertaining Bunkie five consecutive hours, beginning with an hour of her favorite game show. *However* . . .

Occasionally, when I was at the bowling alley, Bunkie called me to find out whether the television was broken. That particular call was much more frequent in 1999. Fortunately, the television was never broken. Most often, Bunkie had mistakenly touched a button on the remote panel that disabled all TV functions or either scanned the channels, muted the volume, or turned the set off, and she could not remember how to use the remote features.

After a few minutes of joking with Bunkie to settle her nervousness, I guided her step by step over the phone until she completed the procedure. Once the television was "fixed" to suit her, Bunkie was just happy knowing that the television was not broken.

One time, when she was unable to master using the remote, Bunkie went independent on me and used the main TV set panel. I had started down the hall to my bedroom when she summoned me to return to the den. Whatever Bunkie did in less than a minute took me longer than three hours, with manual in hand, to undo.

The year was 1998. At the time, we had a new television that had several auxiliary features; and knew absolutely nothing about each one of them. Two hours later, I still had not been able to retrieve the basic menu frame, let alone reprogram the channels. Both of us began thinking there had to be a malfunction in need of repair. We also began laughing as I blamed Bunkie jokingly for breaking our new television set. In another hour, I closed the manual, which I evidently could not read with understanding. Pushing every button, separately and in all sorts of combinations, I trial-and-errored myself to success.

The telephone presented a much bigger problem for Bunkie and me. In fact, we concocted an advanced self-help course in "telephone management" just for 1999. We had passed our introductory course about three years earlier after Bunkie consented for a telemarketer to switch over our long-distance carrier to a company of lesser quality. She also agreed for another telemarketer, who represented one of Bunkie's credit card banks, to enroll her in some kind of membership program that added a monthly fee to her credit card bill. Those were two solicitations to which, even a year before, Bunkie would have never consented. The fact that she did was further indication that her judgment was wavering. Luckily, both incidents were discovered before any payment was made.

Pursuing a line of precaution, Part I of our introductory course was short and simple; *Do not talk to telemarketers or other strangers over the telephone.* Part II was *Do not buy anything by telephone.* Part III developed as I overheard Bunkie giving some caller her Social Security number; *Do not give any data about yourself or your daughter to anybody over the phone or in person, especially to strangers. It may cost you in a court of law, or worse. We could both end up in jail!*

Unfortunately, our introductory course was not adequate in preparing us for two future problems that were probably already in the making. One of those problems had an unnecessary financial attachment that needed to be cut immediately. So back to the rack we went to fetch another new spool of adjustment. This new situation of ours required a stronger thread of "thorough persuasion."

Bunkie and I actually began the advanced level of do's-and-don'ts for using the telephone in 1998. Over the first six months of that year, three of our monthly telephone bills topped fifty dollars, which almost tripled our average monthly amount. From the first to the third, the amount per bill was higher in that order.

I handled the first bill without consulting Bunkie. My prediction that she would not admit to knowing anything more than I did about the inflated amount proved true when I talked to her about the second bill that came the next month. We both looked at each other, knowing nothing about the calls that had been billed to us. In fact, Bunkie assured me that she had not made any calls or used the operator. I did not belabor the issue because I knew either denial or forgetfulness had claimed her mind.

Four months later, the third bill provided all the information I needed to make a complete assessment of the situation. We had a bunch of calls on that bill to the tune of almost a hundred dollars. Seventeen of the calls were brief local and long distance operator assisted calls, accounting for more than a third of the amount. About ten more long distance calls were dialed directly and charged for the one-minute minimum rate. But the plot thickened!

Over a four-day period, several of the calls were made on the same day. Except for one digit, most of the telephone numbers called matched those of our relatives and friends. Having determined that the problem was Bunkie constantly dialing the wrong number, the solution was relatively easy; just not soon enough.

Choosing not to ask Bunkie anything about the calls,

I very gently informed her of the new rate increase for calling "Information" and using the operator to assist in making calls. Great emphasis was placed on *Do not use the operator unless you absolutely must!* From that point on, Bunkie usually made all of her calls when I was home, having me dial the numbers for her. Nevertheless, our thread of thorough persuasion lasted just so long.

As far back as the mid-eighties, the "big block number" touch tone telephone became our newest household commodity. In addition to the enlarged numbers, other new features made it easier for Bunkie to make outgoing calls. We proudly designated the first of the programmed call buttons as "my spot." That button was normally programmed with the number for Bunkie to reach me. Whenever I was going to a particular place, I always checked "my spot" to make sure the number to my whereabouts was properly programmed.

Over the next ten years, as Bunkie's Parkinson's worsened, she mistakenly erased telephone numbers that had been programmed for her use. She would also switch the "ring" volume to "off." The increased frequency of those mistakes to three or four times a month created a compound and more involved problem. In the process, there was one more unwanted revelation.

Several times, Bunkie had the operator or our neighbors assist her in reaching me by phone. One day, she got a kick out of bragging about the operator who was kind enough to call every bowling establishment in the Atlanta area because Bunkie could not remember the name of my regular bowling center. Her main purpose, whenever she tracked me down most times, was just to tell me that our telephone was not working. Then, much later in 1999, Bunkie's behavior slightly suggested undisputable fright, disorientation, or agitation when she was unable to operate the phone and, more so, whenever she was unable to reach me.

As a possible solution, my standard practice was to call Bunkie whenever I was away from home longer than an hour, and more than once, depending on how long I was gone. She was always glad and so responsive when I called to check on her. If I called home twice, a few minutes apart, and Bunkie did not answer, I guessed the ringer was off. I simply went home from wherever I was. Eventually, I stopped going to the bowling alley just to practice.

Bunkie and I received an "incomplete" grade in our advanced telephone management course. In the next few months, Alzheimer's teamed up with Parkinson's; they took full charge of our class and forced us to withdraw.

Our final advanced course was the shortest of the three; "Mind Reading." We had less than a year of active enrollment. The need for this course evolved as Bunkie's behavior reached a new height of abnormal preoccupation and repetition.

For a brief number of weeks in 1999, Bunkie asked the time throughout the day, often asking three or four times within ten minutes. Sometimes she skipped a day or two before starting again. Before associating that behavioral tendency with Alzheimer's, I once commented to Bunkie about her constantly wanting to know what time it was. She became a little upset with me and in response, questioned me; "You don't want to tell me what time it is?" Thereafter, I told Bunkie the time a lot of times, every time she asked. I still wondered, however, why she wanted to know what time it was so many times a day; what, exactly, made time such a primary focal point?

Then there was the "pack-rat" episode. Most of the century that Bunkie almost lived, she was a pack rat. The proof was in the old belts and shoes, broken jewelry, expired credit cards, church bulletins, receipts, bill statements, recipes, cancelled checks, and other stuff she had accumulated since her first day on earth, or so it seemed. Bunkie threw nothing away, from the first suitcase she had in the 1930s to the last several lamps that she "shook to death" because of Parkinson's. The most immediate objects that had a ten-year qualifying status for the junkyard included the headboard and the adjoining set of twin beds in her bedroom.

In October of 1999, one day I returned home very hungry and tired from a long day of tournament bowling. I made my hunger well known to Bunkie, whom I located on one of her beds surrounded by big mounds of her paper product keepsakes. Some had been housed under the beds. Some had been emptied from her dresser drawers. As we greeted each other, Bunkie made a pitch for me to help clean up what became six, tall, kitchen size GLAD bags, filled to capacity. I managed to ignore my hunger temporarily. I was satisfied momentarily by knowing that we were about to make a significant contribution to the sanitation pickup truck. But I was not the only one ignoring my hunger.

Bunkie continued to sit, watch and command without giving me a rest period. My next orders included dismantling one of her beds for its long overdue throw out, and changing the linen on the remaining bed. Despite my hunger, I proceeded to do as ordered. Her supervision and add-on tasks during the cleanup and dismantling of the bed were tolerable. But the task of changing the linen became the epitome of slavery. Although I had tended to Bunkie's bed for many years, my experience in making her bed and turning the covers back for her nighttime sleep was totally irrelevant and disregarded.

From the time I unfolded the first sheet to put on the bed, Bunkie indicated a certain way for the sheet to be handled. I was flooded with conflicting orders the rest of the way; first the sheets, next the blankets, and then pillow cases. Essentially, I was repeating her orders in circles while halfway guessing what she wanted done. The only sure thing was that our minutes were turning into hours.

The bed was just about finished, when, out of the blue, Bunkie decided the mattress should be turned. Putting forth every effort not to blemish my record of accommodating my mother's needs, wants, or commands (no matter how odd the latter two request groups), I stripped the mattress and flipped it over.

After beginning anew the process of making the bed and almost finishing again, Bunkie wanted the head-to-toe position of the box spring switched.

That did it! Enough was enough! *I was hungry!* Since the hungrier I got, the more frustration I had to hide from Bunkie, I had no choice but to take control of my destiny.

With visions of dying from starvation, I said to my mother, "Bunkie, your daughter is hungry and needs to eat *now!*"

Bunkie, surprised that I had not eaten, responded candidly and much to my delight: "By all means, honey; you go on and eat. I didn't mean for us to get into this tonight. We could have done all of this another time."

I do not remember whether I was more shocked by my immediate release from three hours of bondage or Bunkie's failure to remember that her persistence had prolonged my hunger. Neither really mattered. But I tarried not a second longer. We were rapidly approaching midnight; it was almost time for another day's breakfast before I had eaten that day's dinner.

Bunkie and I left her bedroom together. She stretched out on the sofa in our den and took a nap. After finally eating, I returned quietly to her room and finished my task with the bed. Bunkie spent the entire night on the sofa. That night was her first of many entire nights on the sofa in the absence of house guests.

The pack-rat episode was significant in helping me realize how extensively Bunkie's thoughts were cluttered with confusion. In the peak times of her confused state of mind, she could not match words with her thoughts. Consequently, I was left with a broad field task of mind reading. Reading between the lines in the height of her confusion was extremely difficult; my best guesses were more wrong than right. In turn, Bunkie became highly irritable because she was not being understood; hence, her frustration was misguided. Since I was the only available target, I became the recipient of her high-powered and frequent verbal blows.

A few times, the side attraction of Bunkie's peak episodes was ransacking her room and accusing me falsely for the disarray. On one of those occasions, she seemed so natural and was so direct as well as overbearing. I was hurt and, out of long suppressed frustration, I retaliated by sassing Bunkie. The fact that she was unable to consciously retain that incident in her memory beyond five or ten minutes never consoled me to this present day.

As we began the last two months of 1999, the thread of interpretation needed to penetrate the new fabric of Bunkie's mind and patch together her words and thoughts or wants was neither long or strong enough. Besides approaching a "thread deficit" of a sort, three more aspects of our continued climb were self-evident: I was definitely flunking our mind-reading course; our rack of new spools of adjustment, for all practical purposes, was exhausted; and Bunkie and I had much more climbing to do from our mountaintop.

In a rare moment of solitude, hope sprang eternal! I recalled something my grandmother said from time to time: "A new broom sweeps good, but the old broom knows where the dirt is."

What a great light bulb and application for Bunkie and me! The newest thing is not always the best or most effective need. Every now and then, regardless of circumstances, all that's needed is the "good old solid stuff" that knows its way to the root of life's unending heartaches and has the power to create substantial relief.

Old Threads of Humor and Friendship

The accessories of human life include an assortment of that good old solid stuff needed for patching the heart, mind, and a broken spirit. Some people find emotional comfort and strength in the sound of a gentle waterfall, while others take delight in watching the dawning of a new day or beholding the beauty of a golden sunset. Workaholics become more absorbed in work, and romantics take a fantasy stroll down memory lane. There is also the soothing impact that comes with a cocktail, fishing, listening to soft jazz, or talking with a best friend. Then, somewhere close to God at the center of some households, there is the awesome sound of laughter from children, elders, and others between; the resounding force of humor itself.

Before that year's end, I brought my personal philosophy into the practical arena; some things in life are not meant to be done alone. That's what friends are really for! Furthermore, in critical moments of gloom and defeat, humor is good. There was peace in knowing that God made all two of those things—friends and humor.

Humor was always a daily thread in our lives. As a matter of fact, I grew up on Pet Milk, grits, and humor. Back to the very early days of our threesome with Mama, any two of us could be easily caught laughing at the third of us. Bunkie, the most recognized prankster among us three, enjoyed laughter, and laughed at herself more than anybody else. She was a pro at creating instant moments of humor; her theatrics in imitating others were outrageously superb. Long before animation was popular in the film industry, Bunkie gave life to B.O. Plenty, a character from the golden era of the "Dick Tracy" comic strip. Anybody would have thought that Bunkie and B.O. Plenty were personal "live" friends, not knowing any better.

Little did I realize that, one day, humor would serve me as an emotional cure. The last two months of 1999, Bunkie wasn't laughing as much on her own anymore. Old threads of humor became effective as our weapon of survival in the battle between Bunkie and Alzheimer's. Anything and everything that we had enjoyed laughing about throughout our years together was brought to the battlefront, not only in our times of peace. Humor was the calming mechanism for Bunkie's peak moments of confusion and irritation. Conversations about our cats or my growing up years, and even B.O. Plenty, partially resuscitated her mind from total disorientation. The minute she laughed was an indication that humor had temporarily stayed the battle.

The only brutal time of day was making preparations to eat. The few times when humor didn't work, Bunkie and I were at the peak of frustration together. The sensation was the same as a storm. We just had to wait it out. I remembered the times from many years before when Mama and I predicted that anything related to eating would be a big problem to handle with Bunkie if she were to ever become disabled. Obviously, any two of us could also be easily caught talking behind the back of the third of us.

Our prediction became a truism in November of 1999. From the point of preparing food for Bunkie until the time she actually ate, the fusion of her former character and abnormal state of mind presented more than a united front. There was the continued irony of Bunkie's eating policy and practice.

As much as Bunkie enjoyed cooking for others and having our relatives and friends dine in our home, seldom was she known to eat away from home. The many times we stopped to stay overnight at a motel, whoever else was in the car and I headed to a restaurant to eat. Bunkie settled down in the room with her common and preferred stock of peanut butter, Vienna sausages, and saltless top crackers. Sometimes she also brought along cake and fried chicken from home. I grubbed from the restaurant and Bunkie's bounty.

On her rare occasions of being downed by a severe case of flu, Bunkie managed to survive on that same infamous diet until she could prepare her meals. She also equally loved and devoured bananas, apples, vanilla ice cream, peanuts, and Mr. Goodbar or Baby Ruth candy. Her main liquid intake on any and every day was water and pineapple juice.

Bunkie completely relieved herself from cooking on a permanent basis in 1996 as more prominent effects of Parkinson's showed up. Lucky me! I became the head chef. Bunkie had taught me to cook when I was a child. Many times in my adult years we cooked side by side, or she directed me as I cooked. So I knew all about her favorite foods and the particulars of how she preferred her food to be cooked. She graciously ate my cooking until November of 1999. On most days that followed, a great portion of my time was spent rewarming and changing her meals throughout the day. First she was hungry, and then she wasn't. Next she fluctuated between wanting this or that, and then she wanted neither. The chore of preparing her food became tiring and was further compounded by the hardship of getting her to eat.

Due to her basic and transient mental state, time was long coming before Bunkie favored or accepted any assistance in being fed. In that respect, her independence was absolute and far stronger than her need to be assisted. Several times, sneaking side glances, I saw my mother quivering from Parkinson's and eating face down in her tin plate. The sight was depressing and painful, yet I knew any action on my part would have added aggravation to what already had to be a discomfort for her. However, with my slight persistence each mealtime, Bunkie allowed me to feed her, but only a few times the rest of that year.

Bunkie's ill-mannered disposition, promoted by dementia, was another factor that prolonged the process of getting her to eat, most times by twenty minutes or longer. She constantly wanted the food arranged on her plate in a certain way. The meat was always the problem. Doubting my emotional survival, a few times I wondered how many different ways and how many times I could turn the same turkey wing, two chicken thighs, or three strips of bacon on the same plate. The answer to myself was always the same: as many times as it takes to satisfy Bunkie. Between her erratic requests and my wrong guesses, I was unable to determine the number of ways to rearrange meat on her plate.

On a day in early December, Bunkie's focus on rearranging her food lasted longer than ever. She was demanding, on and off, for almost an hour before eating. Most befitting for her confused state of mind, the heart of the problem was two chicken sandwiches, each containing a boneless chicken thigh. In the thick of turning the chicken this way and that, our frustration mounted through the roof.

By the time she finally accepted an arrangement of her food, I was upset enough to light up a cigarette in her very presence, but I constrained myself. Instead, I lit one up in my car. The intent was not to conceal my habit. Bunkie knew that I was a cigarette smoker. Since I had chosen to never smoke at home or in her presence, doing so at that particular time would have been a blatant act of disrespect. Stooping to that level of behavior was never a part of our relationship. Furthermore, I would have never been able to wipe such a deliberate and unkind act from my conscience, whether she were in good or poor health.

When I returned from my car a few minutes later, Bunkie said, while unsteadily shaking a chicken thigh in her hand with a genuine smile, "You better come on and have some. It's mighty good!" I doubt that she even remembered our combined state of mind from the half-hour before.

One other time, close to the day of that episode, Bunkie mustered strength enough to throw her food mostly to the floor. Her displeasure was at an all-time high that entire day. Nothing had gone well or right. I went to the bathroom and let the faucet run while I cried. I was tired. I was angry, and for the first time I was beginning to feel the trap of a hopeless situation. I prayed again, rinsed my face and returned to Bunkie. As I began cleaning her dinner from the floor, her words went straight to my heart.

"Thank you for cleaning this up," she said. "It fell before I could catch it."

I pointed to the top of the television and asked with a civil tongue, "The food fell all the way to the top of the television?"

Bunkie responded, "I guess the lady put that up there like that." We both smiled with ease as I retrieved the bacon strip from the TV and finished cleaning.

Following that incident, I decided it was no longer beneficial to prepare our plates together. Mine was often cold by the time I got a chance to eat. In both our best interest, I waited for Bunkie to finish her meal before I ate. I still wonder sometimes why she never wanted her chocolate chip cookies arranged in a certain way, especially since they had become a regular part of her daily diet.

The food-throwing incident was definitely another turning point in our lives; our upward climb had reached a new and lower level. Our thread of humor was ample in length, but becoming frail and in need of a supplement. Bunkie's dementia was on the rise, and my emotional strength was weakening. However, as Bunkie's only caregiver, I could not afford to give up our battle midway into its advanced stage. So of all the good old solid stuff available, I grabbed the best: two old threads of friendship.

Bunkie and I were quite fortunate and richly endowed in the area of friendships. Among my bowling buddies, former colleagues and students, high school classmates, our neighbors, church members, and significant others, we had a tremendous support system in our friends. They were gracious and generous in their response to us. Two of my best friends, Clara and Elaine, probably qualified for ear and shoulder transplants. The more difficult my climb became, the more I relied on the thread of our respective friendship.

My relationship with each of them was longer than thirty years, and begun in similar manner. I met Elaine as a coworker the first year of my professional employment. Clara and I were coworkers during my first year of employment in Atlanta Public Schools. I adopted their families and they adopted Bunkie and me; their husbands became my brothers.

Whether with Clara or Elaine, we were as silly as geese or as serious as world-renowned scholars. They were my confidantes, and by my side from the first day Bunkie and I began our climb. Talking with either was therapeutic; I could sit and say anything or nothing. Between the two of them, I had a haven for brief retreats and a relief "sitter" for Bunkie always on standby. Most of all, in the two of them, I had the presence of God giving me aid; I was sustained through the final step of my climb.

Additional friends from whom I garnered immediate strength and support during the most difficult of my days were Fredericka Hurley and Tom and Poppye Wood, parents whom I adopted years before; Marynette Reid Bolden, a sister borne by the days of our childhood; and my "angel of mercy," in the person of Mary Brinson Robinson.

The Hands of Time

The year of 1999 was hardly modest as the "King of Years" in Bunkie's bout with dementia. It was our record year of challenge, compromise, and sacrifice. Our mountaintop that had been much greener and more plentiful with daily comfort and joy faded faster in the distance of our climb. Amid the continuing onslaught of changes in Bunkie's declining health, our energy was spent reflecting and clinging as long as we could to stability of a life we once knew. But the more we forged ahead in the diseased battle of our climb, the more the hands of time became our handicap, at a tick-tock pace. Ultimately, our primary cause for happiness was getting through another day.

Sudden Impacts

In contrast to the come-and-go peaks of Bunkie's demented episodes, Alzheimer's altered her interests in life with permanence, one by one. Watching TV baseball was one of her favorite leisure activities for many years. From the time the Braves' franchise moved to Atlanta, Bunkie and I eagerly awaited each game to perform our standard duty. Along with Mama, we were self-appointed members of the Braves' unpaid and unrecognized den-sitting coaching staff. When games were aired only on cable TV, we coached with the same enthusiasm via radio. But not so for Bunkie in 1999; the entire baseball season suddenly vanished from her list of priority interests.

The customary fanfare of the Christmas season also lost its appeal. Mailing and receiving Christmas cards was always such a special time for us. Our Christmas card mailing list grew each year. Before mailing our cards, Bunkie checked with me constantly to make sure some relative or friend was not overlooked. If we made a late discovery of forgetting somebody, that person was sure to receive a New Year's card. One year, we were real late; that person got a Valentine's Day card.

As early as 1997, Bunkie almost stopped asking whether Christmas cards had been addressed to various people. But the Christmas of 1999 was the first that she showed very little concern about the few people to whom she routinely sent gift checks. I was quite aware of her recipients and remembered to include a check with their cards. Attempting to raise her interest, I mentioned some of her "gift" recipients while addressing our cards. Bunkie only smiled and said, "Yeah," indicating to me that I should send them a check. I also remembered the amount she wanted given to each person because Bunkie was an "equal opportunity philanthropist."

Each year, following our switch to an artificial Christmas tree, decorating our seven-footer was party time in our living room. As soon as we gathered for the task at hand, Mama and Bunkie sat and talked and waited on my orders while I decorated the tree. Their hard job was handing me various ornaments or trimmings whenever I was caught in an awkward position at the tree. The volume of Christmas carols, as they played on the stereo, was heard throughout our home. Midway some of the carols, we dared join the harmony. At any moment, Bunkie was expected to slip away to the kitchen and prepare snacks for us. Despite all the fun we had, about two hours from the start I always became the sinking ship; Mama and Bunkie abandoned me.

Before the holiday season ended, somewhere on the agenda was our traditional nighttime sightseeing tour through various neighborhoods. We interrupted our sing-along with the radio to rate the scenic displays of Christmas. Most were beautiful; some made us actually slow down and wonder "what the . . ."

During the Christmas of 1999, the tradition that we continued for fifteen years without Mama was broken. For the first time, Bunkie declined our tour and never made her typical comments on our tree. After inviting her a few times to see the tree and give her stamp of approval, she only looked at the tree once. Again, she just uttered, "yeah." But I could tell by her eyes and smile that she was pleased.

When the clock struck midnight on December 31st, in response to our long New Year's hug, Bunkie repeated "Happy New Year" three times.

Alzheimer's also snatched Bunkie's attraction to our pet cats, but far more slowly. Each one had been the center of our attention since arriving in our home. Their little stunts were our daily topic of conversation. The special way in which Bunkie talked to our cats and mocked them was downright pitiful, but hilarious.

Perhaps the most unfortunate event during Bunkie's advanced stage of dementia was losing one of the three remaining "zoo kids," as we called them. PJ died from old age late summer of 1999. Though Bunkie was still attentive to Bandit and Whimper, her interest level changed. She no longer talked and laughed freely about the time she formed a posse to look for Whimper, or the time she brought a dead cat home for burial.

Not that Bunkie and I were often upset with each other, but talking about the cats was our way of breaking the ice when we got on each other's last nerve. That was common practice long before Bunkie was stricken with Alzheimer's. The "posse" and "dead cat" incidents just happened to be among the most reliable in counteracting Bunkie's disorientation and other periods of her irrational behavior.

Whimper was barely five months old when Bunkie took her on a brief ride to the store. As soon as Bunkie opened the car door, Whimper made a quick and unexpected leap onto the heavily driven parking lot. In her distress, Bunkie attracted several people who joined her search for Whimper. Nightfall was near and not the best time to find a small black kitten whose only separation from the dark of night was her narrow white breast line. Luckily, there was the advantage of the parking lot being adequately lit. Within an hour, Whimper was spotted atop a high mound of dirt that was part of a construction area at the shopping plaza. She finally came down to Bunkie, but only after the last stranger who assisted in finding her was totally out of sight.

After that experience, the cats rode in our cars only to go to their vet.

In the second case, about a year later, Bunkie led Mama and me to grieve a dead cat that she picked up one evening several miles from our home. That particular evening was the third day that Star had been AWOL. As we grieved, Star appeared late that night with an injured leg. He arrived in time to see "his twin," another big orange tabby, stretched full length in the casket Bunkie made. Star sniffed around the casket out of curiosity for a hot second before signaling to us that he wanted to go inside the house and bed down for the night.

The dead cat was released to the sanitation department the next day, and Star landed at his vet's office. We laughed at the sound he made while running in our hall with his leg in a cast. He tugged at getting the cast off into the night. Early the next morning, Star awakened me; he was sitting on his hind legs at my shoulder with the whole cast dangling to the side of his leg. Finishing what he could not do, I cut the attached cast from him.

There were enough incidents about our cats to talk and laugh about through all eternity. But Bunkie's interests in the zoo kids dwindled bit by bit.

Loss of interest was just one in a series of sudden impacts that Alzheimer's had on Bunkie's behavior. Newer and different kinds of erratic behavior were still to come. She seemed to gasp for logic as one does unsuccessfully for breath when drowning. There was greater loss of her ability to understand, such as distinguishing between the beginning and end of televised programs. For a few weeks, she was often offended, thinking that I had changed the channel, even if I were in another room. In a few instances, Bunkie was more upset that I wouldn't "turn it (the program) over and get the other part," as she requested. She also talked about "getting the other part" sometimes when she was using the bed pan.

In January of 2000, Alzheimer's started to shred Bunkie's mind into a slew of tiny pieces that almost erased the success of our previous patchwork. Our roles completely reversed; she was the child and I was the parent. Instead of helping her to dress, I was selecting her clothes for the day and completely dressing her. I was also attending to all of her hygienic needs. Though Bunkie never balked at being bathed or cleaned for a diaper change, having her hair combed or teeth brushed, one time she was totally confused about the need to change the way she had dressed herself.

To my surprise, her confused state of mind did not result in a formal rebellion.

Bunkie awakened early one Sunday morning in January and dressed herself for church. She was fully clad with underwear over pajamas, socks pulled halfway over stockings that sagged midway up her legs, and each shoe on the wrong foot. She was so proud of having dressed herself; her expressed intention was "helping" me out. As I thanked her and began removing her clothes, Bunkie persisted in wanting me to understand that she was already dressed for church. Her only focus was on the help she needed to get another pair of shoes over those already on her feet.

I was fairly skilled and successful in drawing Bunkie's attention away from herself long enough to deal with the task at hand. That was a useful tactic to curb her confusion, but not on that Sunday morning. I had been more successful attending her needs when she was agitated than I was that morning. Realizing my reliable tactics were failing, I promoted one of my back-up strategies to strategy number one. By that time, I had a mammoth warehouse of strategies; it was a matter of choosing the right one for the right moment.

I discovered a couple of months before that Sunday morning that leaving Bunkie for ten minutes or a little longer also significantly reduced her level of confusion and other demented states. So I left, hoping as I went and pleased as punch that she was not also irritable during that episode of confusion.

The minute I returned, Bunkie was eager and willing

for me to get her ready for church. She reacted as if that were our first attempt of the morning.

That morning was her one and only time of a Sunday morning episode. From the first Sunday in January until May, Bunkie missed going to church three times, two of which were due to rain. Her last Sunday in attendance was Mother's Day 2000.

Going to church was not only a constant on our "must do" list, it was standard practice and a habitual expectation. Our rare absences from church raised our popularity. Several members would call, automatically concerned that something drastic had happened to us.

The few times we traveled over a weekend, we visited one of our denominational churches for Sunday morning worship. Flint, Michigan was our only place of exception for not attending one of our sister churches. Instead, we visited the Baptist church I attended the year I worked in Flint. Our last visit to Trinity Missionary Baptist Church was in 1978. Some of the members there continued to ask about Bunkie for several years.

Between 1998 and 2000, there were three Sunday mornings I had no intention at all of going to church. I only went because Bunkie wanted to go, and I knew how much being in church on Sunday morning meant to her. On each of those mornings, two to three hours before time to go to church, Bunkie had just been released from an extended overnight emergency ordeal at the hospital. But she was determined and much stronger than the weakling she had for a daughter.

Oddly enough, Bunkie had the presence of mind to devise a system for keeping up with Sundays, which lasted until her last Sunday at church. I was a month catching on to her game plan. By January of 2000, between Tuesday and Saturday each week, she asked on at least three different days, "Bunkie (me), do we go any-where today?" Sometimes she also asked about "tomor-row." But was that not clever or what?

Occasionally, when I indicated that we were not go-ing out that day or the next, her response was one of sheer gladness; "*Good!*" She realized that she would not have to go through the hassle of getting ready. Some of those times, before 2000, she was still able to dress herself.

Any paraphrase of "getting ready" also evolved with sentimental value.

Bunkie was known for making a standard announce-ment of her readiness when we were about to eat, go out, or bed down for the night. This news flash began initially as her way of mocking me when I was a child. Modified in later years, it was still short and simple; "Bunkie (to me), I'm ready."

In the nineties, if we were going out, Bunkie didn't just stop with her announcement; she strutted herself as a model, tall and proud. Due to her case of Parkinson's, dressing herself was approaching an act of hard labor.

The times she accompanied me as a guest, Bunkie found delight in being the first of us dressed. She never wanted to slow me down if the trip were a plan or obliga-tion of mine. When the trip was hers, it didn't matter who was the first dressed or when we actually walked out of the door.

Bunkie was equally dutiful in mandating when we should begin our preparations even if we were just think-ing about shampooing our hair; "Bunkie (to me), let's get ready." Other times, she would say, "Time to get ready." Either way, it was the last thing I wanted to hear if I were taking a much needed nap or just plainly didn't need to go wherever or do whatever.

Early one Monday morning in November of 1999,

"Let's get ready," took on new meaning for both of us. I was preparing to go to my bowling league, and Bunkie was still in bed, but awake. A common practice in our household was always for the first person awake and up to greet the other(s) for the day. On that particular Monday morning, Bunkie and I had gone through that ritual. But the usual talking we did while I dressed wasn't happening. Since both of us were late night people, I thought Bunkie was having one of her sleepier mornings; that is, until I went into her room for our good-bye hug.

No sooner than our embrace, Bunkie said with reluctance in her soft voice, "I guess we better get ready." Neither of us smiled that time. Her news flash that always had the same meaning, regardless of words added or deleted, was somehow different. We never spoke of why we were getting ready; the unexpected suddenness of the announcement and the sudden difference in her voice said it all. Instead of going to the bowling alley, I drove Bunkie to the emergency room. We would make the same trip six more times, including two on my bowling mornings.

Bunkie continued her mockery of me with "Let's get ready" as an expression of fun, and sometimes as a need for emergency medical assistance. I never had to wonder which time was which. Her voice alone declared the difference, but never as an alarm. Over time, I developed a sense of parental intuition; Bunkie was well on her way to becoming my child, and I, her parent.

The turn for announcing our readiness recycled to me on June 14, 2000. Late on that afternoon, forcing my emotional pain behind a smile, I stroked my mom's face and gently said, "Bunkie, let's get ready." Without any hesitation, Bunkie replied, "Yeah." I called for an ambulance.

That day was the last time of our homemade broadcast to each other. In that fleeting moment of finality, we also set another record to file in Bunkie's archives. June 14, 2000 was the first time ever that Bunkie agreed to medical attention at my request. I felt so accomplished!

Profiles of a Magical Nap

Caring for Bunkie full time as her life was being reordered constantly by Alzheimer's became more than a one-way irreversible climb. We endured the challenges of multiple descending levels and phases. Throughout our experience, there was neither a map nor tour guides; just the two of us as first-time tourists. The thick of our climb had no exit ramps to rest stops; just the day-to-day commotion of a disease distorting Bunkie's mental faculties and my faked suppression of emotional strain derived from not knowing what bizarre behavior was ahead. We were also faced with the uncertainty of whether a time would come when we would no longer share the iota of mutual sensibility and understanding to which we had grown accustomed in our most recent years together.

Though Alzheimer's advanced with notorious precision in robbing Bunkie's mind, her character was amended in 2000 with a trait altogether foreign to her personality. Effects of that impact extended the mystery of her diseased mind.

Prior to being afflicted with dementia, the range of Bunkie's expletives was limited to four terms: "darn," "shoot," "shucks," and "for Pete's sake." Profanity had never been used by either of us in our home. Bunkie always spoke at home and away with a guarded tongue. She was so morally and motherly fit and sound that she didn't say "pregnant" in my presence until I was fully grown; all pregnant people were "PG," according to Bunkie.

In view of her "clean mouth" record, naturally I would be absolutely shocked to ever hear Bunkie use a curse word. She didn't know how; she was inexperienced; cursing was not her forte. About mid-February, dementia changed all that. I was absolutely shocked! Bunkie cussed! She actually uttered the word reserved by many for use when they stump a toe. Without apparent reason, other than dementia, Bunkie said the "S" word and said it with passion from the start. For the next four months, several times a day in one-minute time blocks, Bunkie, my mother, said the "S" word; sometimes in repeat formation, the induction of an echo.

Bunkie's usage of the "S" word created quick conversions of her warm personality to the cold image of a dictator. Most times her new choice word was used as a destination for me: "Go to S!" That profane comment was a regular entry during our conversations. Sometimes it was a response and sometimes not; it was just an unrelated, out-of-the-blue statement. A couple of times as we talked about a program while watching it on TV, Bunkie suddenly looked at me and blurted, "Go to S!" Surprisingly one night, that was her response to my "Good night."

As usual, I waited until her mental comeback. Before going to bed that night, Bunkie said to me, "Good night, Bunkie." Saying good night in our home was also a standard practice that never went undone, dementia or not.

Usually I was not disturbed by this latest show in Bunkie's sequence of demented behaviors. Every now and then I said to her, "Bunkie, bring my mother back 'rat' now!" Sometimes that was all it took to get her back. But a few times that appeared to be the least of her demented moments, the mandate was so deliberate and malicious that I was caught completely off guard; I took her offensive mood personally. Of course, the minutes I spent in agony and being frustrated on those few occasions proved a perfect waste of my emotional energy and time, simply because of her memory span. Five minutes later, Bunkie was unaware of her offense, and moving on with life in a much kinder mood.

Nevertheless, I cried two times, but again, not in her presence. One of those times, I sought solace in the bathroom (again). In addition to letting the faucet run, I also flushed the toilet twice to make sure that my wailing was not overheard. The second time occurred in April at church during the pastoral prayer. I left Bunkie's side and made a blanket response to her years of Alzheimer's with my tears. A short while later, I returned and decided to sit elsewhere. Bunkie and I hugged after the service. We also enjoyed each other during our ride home and for the rest of that day.

Instead of crying the remaining few times when dementia coated Bunkie's expression of the "S" word with cruelty, I chose a live target and vented directly. No person qualified better to serve in that role than my sisterly friend, Elaine. Each time, as soon as I grabbed a bit of privacy, I phoned her. Without the courtesy of a "Hello," I instantly blurted for her to "go to 'S'!" Knowing and understanding my plight, Elaine retorted with the same compassion and the same comment. We talked until one of us made the other laugh; then I was okay (again).

Besides familiarity with Bunkie's illness, Elaine had a special and dear relationship with Bunkie. One of their most laughed about experiences occurred at the Greyhound bus station when they went to pick up Bunkie's stepsister.

In a rare haste of getting dressed, Bunkie forgot to put on a slip. She discovered her lapse upon arriving at the bus station. Standing barely five feet and ninety pounds, Elaine was Bunkie's human shield. Bunkie, a hundred pounds heavier and a foot taller, tried concealing herself by walking closely behind Elaine; portraying a similar weight and height spectacle as the Mutt & Jeff comic duo. Bunkie was more self-conscious than anything; her dress was hardly a see-through. Had it been so, her already inadequate "shield" surely would have been insufficient; she had only a front shield and, definitely, not a baby's backside.

After several weeks of Bunkie's persistence with the "S" word, I labeled each future instance of that behavior as the "S-episode." If ever she prolonged the S-episode more than five minutes with "demented" hostility, I gave her a "time out" to herself. I knew she wouldn't be long before calling out to me by our shared nickname: "Bunkie, whatcha doing?"

I was always relieved when we reached that point, because we were usually good for the next four to six hours. Peace prevailed!

Until June 23, 2000, I was the only known receiver of Bunkie's S-command. But on that day, using the "A" word for the first time and in an unusually loud voice, she issued a brand new collective kissing order to everybody in her hospital room. Our relatives and friends stayed put while I quickly and quietly slipped out of her room; thereby, exercising my brief routine of escape from the unpleasant face of "reality dementia."

That episode was perhaps the worst display of Bunkie's unnatural verbal abuse. Two other possible examples of behavior common to Alzheimer's, that I sometimes shuddered just thinking about, never happened in Bunkie's case.

Once, during her final hospitalization, when Bunkie really didn't want to cooperate with whatever needed to be done, she kicked a nurse in the chest. That action was also her last physical attempt to come home. For that combined reason, Bunkie spent three days restrained to her bed as a precaution. Though she had been less physically threatening on two occasions prior to going to the hospital, Bunkie was never uncontrollably violent.

Bunkie also never strayed from home or lost her way from any other place. Home was where she always wanted to be until her final twenty-four hours.

Of all the behaviors Bunkie did exhibit, none matched the impact of her sudden and complete withdrawal from reality. There were two major occurrences. The manner in which she confused the first incident was a blessing to both of us. The second occurrence could have been an emotional disaster, but was erased by what I will remember forever as a magical nap.

On February 9, 2000, while driving home from a dental appointment, I was a victim in a six-car wreck on one of our busiest and most unsafe highway connectors (Georgia 400). Earlier that day, Bunkie and I attended a funeral. I dropped her off at home and continued to my dentist, comfortably feeling that I would be home within two hours. That decision was one of two good things regarding the wreck. The second was having my seat belt on. I sustained minor discomfort in my neck that lasted about a week. Bunkie was not always the best passenger in the world for wearing a seat belt properly; she constantly tugged at it or held it loosely away from her neckline. I was just happy all of the "could haves" didn't.

The worst of the wreck was my car being practically a

pile of crushed metal, plastic, and glass. The time taken to deal with the wreck exceeded four hours because of the rush-hour traffic. The scene of the accident being a mile from the interstate ramps was an added hindrance.

Realizing that I would get home no time soon, I called Bunkie first, hoping that none of the incident had been reported on TV news. I explained very calmly and even cheerfully what had happened, wanting her to at least sense that I was okay. My next call was to Elaine. The best thing, at that time, was our homes were less than two minutes driving distance apart. Our arrangement was for her to get to my home and stay with Bunkie while her husband, Thomas, also Tom among friends, came to pick me up.

Less than ten minutes later, I called home again. Knowing Elaine, I felt that she was either already at my home or on her way. I also knew Bunkie would not make any kind of response to anybody at our door unless first hearing a voice that she recognized very well. My purpose was alerting Bunkie to expect Elaine.

Learning during the call that Elaine was, in fact, with Bunkie took all my cares away. There would be sufficient light in our home. Bunkie could eat or change TV programs if she wanted and be assisted if she needed to go to the bathroom.

Just for the sake of Bunkie hearing my voice, I called home one more time about an hour later. I thought the sound of my voice would dismiss any anxiety Bunkie may have had about the wreck and me. But things were going much better than I imagined. In addition to Bunkie and Elaine enjoying each other's company, Bunkie had received two phone calls. In both instances, Bunkie informed the caller that I was not home because I was waiting on my dentist; the dentist was running late due to an automobile wreck he had on his way from a funeral. There in the middle of the commotion going on around me, I had a long overdue, hardy laugh.

Life was beautiful! Bunkie had the presence of a daughter in Elaine and was, contrary to my thought, hardly concerned about the wreck or my physical status. Also, my ordeal at the site of the accident ended with perfect timing. Tom and the wreckers arrived just as the police were finally finishing their investigation. The entire experience was nothing short of Divine intervention in its purest form.

Bunkie never talked about the wreck as if I were involved. She never consciously missed my car from our carport, though it was at the dealership two months for repairs.

That wreck was the less serious of two that affected us. In 1974, a drunk off-duty cop sped through a red light and totaled three cars, including mine. I was also the lone passenger in my car at that time.

Unlike Bunkie's reaction to the first wreck, her failure to grasp reality of my 2000 wreck confirmed that Alzheimer's had collapsed her mind into another space and time. Otherwise, from the time of my first call home, Bunkie would have found her way to me out of parental urgency. That was her former sacrificial nature as my mother. As her daughter, I was also sure that Bunkie never detached subconsciously from a sense of motherhood; the proof never escaped her eyes. Alzheimer's only dismantled her parental performance from a conscious level.

Brief preludes to Bunkie's second major episode of active withdrawal began in 1999. Upon awakening from a nap one evening in late summer, she asked, "Where is Mama?" Almost in the same breath, however, she indicated that she was not fully awake at the time she spoke; and even laughed at herself for asking about Mama.

In a similar situation a month or so later, she wanted to know whether Evelyn was gone. As soon as I asked if she were talking about Mrs. Hood, a friend of ours, and a fellow church member, Bunkie realized her lapse of awareness and corrected herself as she wondered, "Why did I ask that?" Though we were family friends, Mrs. Hood did not frequent our home, except for matters of urgency.

A few months later, Bunkie was not as quick in regaining awareness. She wanted to know if "Secret Pal" was still in the other room. To make sure of whom she was speaking, I asked if she were referring to Mrs. Hood. They had called each other Secret Pal since Bunkie's former membership in the same church club with Mrs. Hood. Bunkie confirmed her references without additional dialogue. However, when she spoke in the next few minutes, she had recovered a sense of awareness. That was the first time she did not relate the oddness of her query to her coming out of a sleep; she offered no corrective commentary on the matter.

There were only two more episodes of Bunkie asking about persons who had no active presence in our home. Both times were in December. Each lasted about a minute and followed the pattern of occurring immediately after awakening from a nap. The episodes never happened in her waking hours after a night's sleep, only after a nap.

In the first of the two episodes, Bunkie asked about Mama again. In the second case, she also asked where I was. I immediately said, "huh?" Bunkie quickly indicated that she must have spoken while still half-asleep. I agreed, knowing better.

An experience in January (2000) really got my attention.

Atlanta was paralyzed by its worst ice storm in over half a century. For three days and nights, my immediate neighborhood was without power in subfreezing temperatures. The situation lasted longer in other communities. Luckily, we had use of our telephone. The cloudy, short days and long nights of winter did not allow us much daylight, especially with our home being shaded by trees. We burned a lot of candles.

After my first night of freezing, I made reservations for Bunkie and me at the Ramada Inn. Bunkie agreed to our plan initially, but reneged later. I pursued reservations for the sake of Bunkie's comfort, but I was the one in grave need. She was content with just her pajamas and two blankets on our sofa. I had on double and triplicate clothing with gloves and quilts and went to my car several times each day and night of the ice storm for warmth.

Elaine and Tom were spared from the power outage and invited us to their home. Bunkie chose to remain at our home. Elaine sent us an ample supply of her delicious homemade soup and a quantity of a peach drink. We feasted on that menu the last two days. Bunkie added her favorites of ice cream, crackers, and Vienna sausages. The more ice cream she ate, the more I froze.

On the second evening of the ice storm, as I attempted to assist Bunkie in walking to the bathroom, she pushed me away, saying that she did not know me. I disregarded her comment, and she shoved me from her; but I walked closely behind her as she struggled in her walk to the bathroom. Once there, she recognized me and accepted all my help. I blamed her disorientation on the continuous, dark coldness in our home and her slightly impaired vision.

Several times after the ice storm incident, I recalled a conversation from 1996 with one of our younger family friends, Ronnie. He was raised by his grandmother, who at the time was in her nineties. Ronnie shared with me his devastating experience of not being recognized by "Big Mama," the name by which our families called his grandmother. I often wondered how I would handle such a situation emotionally. What if, one day, Bunkie didn't recognize me for hours at a time, as Big Mama was doing?

I was faced with the reality of that situation mid-April (2000), and it all began at the end of a nap.

In the most emphatic tone possible, Bunkie asked me, "Where is Carole?" The minute she said "Carole," I knew that episode would be different from any other in the past. Something different was happening with her mind. Bunkie normally used my given name in serious times. Whatever the cause, for the next three hours, she never referred to me as Bunkie, only as "Carole" or "my daughter."

I did think, however, that since the other episodes had been brief, the same would be true in that instance. I reacted accordingly. Her previous episodes were probably the reason I didn't outright panic.

The more Bunkie denied my presence as her daughter, the more I tried to amuse her mind back, repeating statements as, "Bunkie, this is me, your daughter. See my face. This face is the only one in the world that looks like yours, because you reproduced it." I continued with those and similar lines on and off for an hour, getting nowhere fast. I even held Whimper to her. She accepted Whimper, but still did not recognize me.

At another point, I moved nearer to Bunkie. She raised her arms, threatening to hit me. I retreated quickly to my chair four feet away and finished the task of dealing with my newly shampooed hair. Meanwhile, Bunkie continued attempts to put on her stockings; she was preparing to go out and search for me. "I'm going and find my daughter," she said forcefully, while looking at me as a stranger.

My energy during those long three hours was not spent primarily despairing her inability to recognize me. My focus was on doing something to jolt her mind with a wave of awareness. However, I was concerned about how I would restrain her physical attempts to leave. I probably would have patronized her efforts had it not been close to one o'clock that night. Warning Bunkie about the lateness of the night had no impact on her determination to find me whatsoever.

Bunkie's newly found strength was a little frightening. Dementia undoubtedly provided her with a different kind of spur-of-the-moment strength. Facing the dilemma of keeping her in the house with that added strength against me brought to memory an incident of just a few weeks earlier.

A health professional visited our home to evaluate Bunkie's need for physical therapy. That assessment was made in conjunction with her Parkinson's. Determined not to be bothered with outside help in our home, Bunkie moved her arms and legs in all kinds of ways and actually stood and pranced a few steps unassisted.

At the time of her evaluation, Bunkie's difficulty in walking had increased tremendously over several months and was getting worse by the week. The same was true of her ability to stand and sit on her own. Physical therapy would have been ideal, considering Bunkie's twenty-year choice to move around mostly out of necessity.

Bunkie's demonstration of physical greatness disqualified her for that therapeutic service. I knew not to even open my mouth in contention. Bunkie could have floored the physical therapist and me at the rate she was moving around. Her adrenalin was in motion!

But that was *then,* and *now* was the night of the nap and my dilemma. Finally, the thought of how stupid I was for ever beginning to consider the possibility of Bunkie going anywhere crossed my mind. She could no longer move herself from the sofa without assistance, let alone take a step. *Aha!* The time for appeasing and patronizing her attempts was upon me one more time. *Let the search begin!*

I tricked Bunkie into letting me comb her hair before going out into the dark of night. I really thought, somehow, familiarity with my voice and combing her hair would restore her awareness. *YEAH!* Bunkie consented and enjoyed herself; her itchy scalp was being scratched free of charge. I made sure to comb her hair a long time, and still got nowhere fast with my goal. When I finished with her hair, Bunkie resumed her preparations to go and search for me. As she fumbled with her stockings, I thought up strategy number 4,513.

The possibility of that Strategy being successful had great merit. My hope was that the sound of somebody else's voice would induce her into a mental comeback. So I began talking about Gambrell, one of her church sons who knew about her mental decline. Bunkie was quick in recognizing him by name. Progress was on the rise!

I called Gambrell. As he and Bunkie talked, he must have commented to Bunkie about me. In turn, she told Gambrell, "Yeah, it's a lady sitting here in the chair, but I don't know her; I'm going and find Carole."

Next, I called Elaine. Her voice had the same effect: *None!* Almost two hours had passed.

Some time in the third hour, after sitting with her face resting in her hands on her lap for a while, Bunkie stretched out on the sofa. My inner stress diminished more significantly. I knew she would soon be asleep. When she began snoring a few minutes later, I left quietly to put away my hair stuff in my bedroom. I was gone about three minutes.

As I returned to the den, Bunkie raised her head, looked around at me and asked, "Bunkie, where have you been?" My response, with a great sigh of relief, was "Welcome back, Kotter!"

Bunkie recalled everything she said and did during her memory lapse. She thought the incident was funny, laughing more because she could not remember any of my reaction, just hers.

Whether a pattern of dementia or not, from that point and for anybody concerned about how weird Alzheimer's is, I had a qualifying example.

Sleep evidently played an incidental role in Bunkie's case of dementia. At any given time in her wakening moments from a nap, her functional power of awareness was either impeded or corrected. The gratifying difference in her two-nap episode was the magic of the second nap in leading her mind back to us. Within her rousing moments, Bunkie remembered that I was her child.

A mother's failure to recognize her child has to be the highest peak of dementia and the lowest time in the life of that child, and in some cases, the most devastating. As Bunkie's adult child, that three-hour failure influenced my final reality check. I, thereby, retired her mind with a personalized title of distinction: "Bunkie Emeritus."

Dementia, in its many forms, is cruel and unique in breaking down one's character. Yet, as overpowering as Alzheimer's was in changing, debilitating, and robbing

Bunkie's mind, she maneuvered a sense of spiritual alignment and naturally so. Her bond with God was unbreakable because the hands of time were God's hands in motion.

As far as I knew, the night of the magical nap in 2000 was the last time Bunkie failed to recognize her one and only child. She transcended to her final destination in a different kind of nap that same year on July 3rd.

In the sense that "life is but a dream," a memory is but the reality of one's destiny in life. Bunkie and I shared the dream of life because that was our destiny. The mountain of dementia was an isolated hand dealt from the deck of life. Bunkie and I gave the climb our best shot!

Finishing Unfinished Business

From a caregiver's perspective, dementia is a formal affair of the mind with a lopsided profile. There is no before and after, only before and during. The challenges are many and vary from day to day. They exhaust one's emotional, physical, and spiritual fortitude. But once human existence is paired with God's governance of natural and universal order, therein created is a base for inner strength and endurance. Each step of my survival was a testament to who God is and what He does in the miracles and tragedies of life.

My climb with Bunkie during her years of Alzheimer's represents only one case of the masses. Hopefully, the presentation of *Bunkie Emeritus* serves its purpose as a source of exposure, inspiration, and strength for those directly and indirectly involved with the plight of dementia.

Afterthought

Personal opinion suggests the human mind in its most normal state bears an individual strangeness that borders abnormality. For that reason, nobody is far removed from the possibility of becoming afflicted with a mental disorder. The pursuit of this author, therefore, embraced the passionate hope that the prospect of preventing Alzheimer's and other mental illnesses will soon become a reality.